Table of Contents

W9-AZW-441

Ancient Babylonia 2-3
Ancient China 4-5
Ancient Egypt 6-7
Ancient Greece 8-9
Ancient Rome 10-11
The Decathlon 12-13
The World Series 14-15
Stanley Cup 16-17
Leonardo da Vinci 18-19
Raphael 20-21
Rembrandt 22-23
Vincent Van Gogh 24-25
Johann Sebastian Bach 26-27
Wolfgang Amadeus Mozart 28-29
Frederic Chopin 30-31
Peter Tchaikovsky 32-33
The Typewriter 34-35
The Telescope 36-37
The Hot-Air Balloon 38-39
The Television 40-41
The Jet Engine 42-43
The Space Shuttle 44-45
The Computer 46-47
The Laser 48-49
The Pyramids 50-51
The Hanging Gardens of Babylon 52-53
The Temple of Artemis at Ephesus 54-55
The Statue of Zeus at Olympia 56-57
The Lighthouse of Alexandria 58-59
The Colossus of Rhodes 60-61
The Mausoleum at Halicarnassus 62-63
The Acropolis 64-65
Stonehenge 66-67
The Great Wall of China 68-69
Angkor Wat 70-71
Modern Wonder: Eiffel Tower 72-73
Taj Mahal 74-75
Suez Canal 76-77
Panama Canal 78-79
The Brooklyn Bridge 80-81
Yellowstone National Park 82-83
Carlsbad Caverns 84-85
Mount Rushmore National Memorial 86-87
The Sequoia 88-89
Niagara Falls 90-91
Antarctica 92-93
Mount Everest 94-95
The Sahara 96-97
The Amazon River 98-99
Easter Island 100-101
Answer Key 102-127

Think About:

Ancient Babylonia

One of the oldest civilizations on Earth was located in an ancient region called Babylonia. This ancient civilization lasted over 2000 years. It was located around the Tigris and Euphrates Rivers in an area that is today called Iraq.

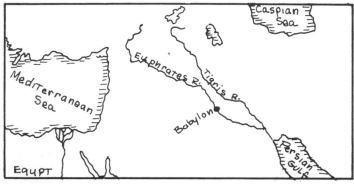

The Babylonian civilization centered around the ancient city of Babylon. Babylon, which means "gate of god," was the cultural, religious and trading center of Babylonia. The city was divided in half by the Euphrates River. Huge walls decorated with blue bricks and paintings of mythical beasts surrounded the city. Large bronze gates allowed people to enter and leave the city.

Babylon was a magnificent city. It contained many palaces and temples. The most famous was the temple of Bel Marduk, the patron god of Babylon. Inside the temple area stood the famous Tower of Babel. Located nearby were the Hanging Gardens of Babylon. The gardens were considered to be one of the Seven Wonders of the World. The gardens were grown on the roof of a large building. The roof was vaulted, or slanted. People used this as a shady, cool area to escape the heat.

The Babylonians worshipped thousands of gods. There were gods and goddesses for practically everything in their lives.

Many Babylonians were farmers. They learned to drain swamps, and more importantly, to irrigate land. They built a series of canals to carry water from the Tigris and Euphrates Rivers to the fields. Because of this, they were able to grow an abundance of vegetables, fruits and grains.

The Babylonians were excellent craftsmen. They learned to make sun-dried bricks which were painted and glazed to decorate buildings. They made elaborate carvings and statues and designed beautiful jewelry of silver and gold.

The Babylonians were one of the first civilizations to develop a system of writing. They used this to record their history, literature, scientific studies and religious texts.

The Babylonians were ruled by many great rulers. One ruler, Hammurabi, developed a set of laws for his people. Today, these famous laws are known as the Code of Hammurabi.

• From what you have read in the story, draw a picture showing how the city of Babylon may have looked. (optional)

Babylonia

Name_____

One of the oldest civilizations on Earth was located in an ancient region

called _____.

The Babylonian civilization lasted over 2000 / 5000 years.

Babylonia was located around the _____ and _____ Rivers

in an area that is today called China. / Iraq.

The Babylonian civilization centered around the ancient city of _____.

✱ Write, check, circle.

Babylon

⤷ . . . means "_____ of _____.

⤷ . . . was the ☐ cultural ☐ dining center of Babylonia.

⠀⠀⠀⠀⠀⠀⠀⠀⠀⠀☐ religious ☐ trading

⤷ . . . was divided in half by the Tigris / Euphrates River.

⤷ . . . was surrounded by a wall decorated with blue bricks / jewels

and paintings of kings and gods. / paintings of mythical beasts.

Babylon contained many palaces / deserts and mountains. / temples.

The most famous was the temple of _____, the patron god of
Babylon.

Inside the temple area stood the famous ☐ statue of Venus. ☐ Tower of Babel.

Located in Babylon was one of the _____ Wonders of the World.

It was called the _____ of Babylon.

Underline the sentence that tells what the Babylonians used their system of
writing to record. (underline directly on the story page).

✱ Write, check.

One of the greatest rulers of Babylonia was _____.

Hammurabi developed a set of ☐ temples. ☐ laws.

Today, these famous laws are known as the _____ of _____.

Think About:

Ancient China

The Chinese civilization is one of the oldest civilizations on Earth. It is believed to have begun over 4000 years ago.

The ancient Chinese were ruled by dynasties, a series of rulers from the same family.

The first known dynasty was the Shang Dynasty. Archeologists have found primitive writing on bones which tells of this culture, which existed over 3000 years ago. The Shang Dynasty was defeated by warriors from a new dynasty called the Chou.

The Chou Dynasty ruled China almost a thousand years. During this time, many local governments were formed throughout China. They fought constantly among themselves for power to rule certain parts, or provinces, of the country. The Chou Dynasty was replaced by the Ch'in Dynasty.

The Ch'in Dynasty broke down many of the local governments and set up one central government for the entire country. The Ch'in Dynasty was ruled by Shih Huang Ti, the first great Chinese dictator. He is famous for building the Great Wall of China, which still stands today. The Ch'in Dynasty was replaced by the Han Dynasty.

The Han Dynasty controlled China for 400 years. During this time, Chinese culture developed rapidly. Art and sciences were valued and education was encouraged. After the Han Dynasty, China broke into many different warring states. This lasted for over 400 years.

Life in these ancient dynasties was different for each class of people. The Emperor lived in the capital city in splendid style. His home was a palace of many rooms, filled with gardens and courtyards.

The people were separated into groups, such as merchants, who sold or traded goods; artisans, who made tools and ornaments; and soldiers.

The peasants made up the largest group of people. They produced the food for the country. Their lives were simple and often very hard. Most peasants lived in tiny, bare houses.

The ancient Chinese produced beautiful works of art. Ornaments and statues were often made of jade. Jade was called "the stone of heaven." The green stone was a symbol of wealth and power.

Painting became a popular art form during the Han Dynasty. Artists painted on wood, silk and paper.

Chinese musicians played instruments similar to our harp, flute and cymbals.

The ancient Chinese developed one of the earliest forms of writing. They first wrote on bones or bamboo. Later they made paper which was used to make books. The Chinese made the first dictionary over 2000 years ago!

Optional
• Draw a time line showing the dynasties of ancient China in the correct order.

China

Name_____

Underline.

The Chinese civilization...

    is believed to have begun over 4000 years ago.

    is believed to have been ruled by 4000 rulers.

> circle one

Check.

The ancient Chinese were ruled by ☐ presidents ☐ dynasties.

The word **dynasty** means...

    ☐ a group of warriors.

    ☐ a series of rulers from the same family.

} check the correct box(es).

Write and check.

The first Chinese dynasty was the _____ Dynasty.

The Shang Dynasty...

    ☐ existed over 5000 years ago.

    ☐ is known because of primitive writing found on bones.

} check the correct box(es).

The Shang Dynasty was replaced by the _____ Dynasty.

The Chou Dynasty...

    ruled China for almost a _____ years. *← Fill in*

    ruled during a time of many ☐ princes ☐ local governments that

    controlled ☐ dynasties ☐ provinces of the country.

} check the correct boxes.

The Chou Dynasty was replaced by the _____ Dynasty.

The Ch'in Dynasty... **(check the correct boxes).**

    ☐ tore down the temples and built new ones.

    ☐ broke down the local governments and set up one central
        government for the entire country.

    was ruled by the first great Chinese dictator, named _____,

    who was responsible for building ☐ the Great Wall of China.
                                ☐ strong armies.

True or False (T or F)

_____ The Chinese emperors lived in splendid style in castles.

_____ Most Chinese people lived in castles.

_____ The Chinese produced beautiful works of art.

_____ The Chinese called diamonds, "the stones of heaven."

_____ Jade was a symbol of wealth and power.

_____ The Chinese played instruments much like our piano.

_____ The Chinese developed one of the earliest forms of writing.

Think About:

Ancient Egypt

Ancient Egypt was one of the most fascinating civilizations in history. The ancient Egyptians were a creative and intelligent people.

Ancient Egypt was located along the Nile River. Most of the land in that area was dry and sandy, which made farming difficult. But the soil along the Nile River was black and rich. Egyptian farmers were able to grow crops in this rich soil.

Egyptians wore light clothing because the climate was so warm. Both men and women wore make-up. Egyptian art shows that they especially used black lines of make-up around their eyes. Many Egyptians wore rings, bracelets, beads and wide jeweled collars. It was common for Egyptians to dye their hair with henna, a red dye.

The Egyptians spoke a language made of several other languages. No one knows how their language sounded. They developed a way of writing their language in picture symbols called hieroglyphics. Hieroglyphic carvings on tombs and monuments have been recovered from ancient ruins by archeologists.

Most of the Egyptians built their cities along the Nile River. The most famous cities of ancient Egypt were Memphis and Thebes.

Memphis was the first capital of Egyptian government. Later, the capital was moved to Thebes. The Egyptians had a sacred burial ground near Thebes called the Valley of the Tombs of the Kings.

The ancient Egyptians were very religious. They believed that they would go to another life after death. To prepare for that life, many rulers, called pharaohs, had huge tombs built and filled with great riches, food and clothing. The Egyptian pyramids are the most famous burial tombs from ancient Egypt. Perhaps the most famous discovery of modern times was the tomb of King Tutankhamon, which was discovered in the Valley of the Tombs of the Kings in 1922.

The civilization of ancient Egypt lasted about 2,500 years before it was conquered by invading armies. Historians believe that Egypt was conquered because it could not defend itself against armies which fought with iron weapons. Much of the civilized world had developed sources of iron. This period was known as the Iron Age. Without iron weapons, Egyptian armies were unable to defend their country.

• Find out when, how and by whom the Egyptian civilization was conquered.

Egypt

Write and check.

Ancient _____ was built along the ☐ Nile ☐ Amazon River.
1→

Match.

Most soil in Egypt. . .   was rich and black.
The soil along the Nile . . .   was dry and sandy.

Write and check.

The ancient Egyptians

Ancient

. . .wore _____ clothing, because the
2→
climate was so warm.

. . .wore _____, especially
3→
around their eyes.

. . .wore ☐ rings   ☐ bracelets
       ☐ crowns   ☐ bonnets
       ☐ beads   ☐ jeweled collars

. . .often dyed their hair red with _____.
4→

The ancient Egyptians wrote in picture symbols, called _____.
5→

The two most famous cities of ancient Egypt were _____
6 →

and _____.
7→

Rulers in Egypt were called _____.
8→

```
          1→ E
     2→      g
5→           y
   3→      -  p
        9→    t
   6→         i
      8→      a
   4→         n
7→            s
```

True or False

_____ The ancient Egyptians were very religious.

_____ The ancient Egyptians believed in life after death.

_____ The ancient Egyptians built tombs as extra rooms in which to keep their possessions.

_____ The pharaohs built tombs and filled them with riches to take to the next life.

_____ The pyramids were built for soldiers to live in.

_____ The pyramids are the most famous burial tombs from ancient Egypt.

Write.

One of the greatest discoveries of modern times was the tomb

of King _____.
9→

Think About:

Ancient Greece

Ancient Greece was one of the most important civilizations in history. It existed over 2000 years ago.

The ancient Greeks developed democracy, a way of life that allowed the people to take part in their own government. This form of government was much different from other cultures of that time, which were ruled by kings and emperors.

Ancient Greece had two main cities, Sparta and Athens.

Life in Sparta emphasized physical activities. Young boys were trained in gymnastics and other sports. Although most Spartans grew into strong adults, they were usually uneducated. Very few Spartans could read or write.

Life in Athens was much different from life in Sparta. The Athenians believed in developing the mind as well as the body. They learned mathematics, literature, writing and music, as well as gymnastics. Individuals were encouraged to develop their own talents. Athens became the center of Greek culture.

The ancient Greeks lived simply. They built their homes of stone and brick around open courtyards.

The Greeks ate only two meals a day. The morning meal was called **ariston.** It consisted of beans or peas. The night meal, called **deipnon,** was a large meal of cheese, olives, bread and meat.

The Greek men and women wore cloaks and sandals.

The people of ancient Greece worshipped many different gods. The chief god, Zeus, was believed to live on Mount Olympus. Zeus was considered the ruler of all other gods and goddesses, such as: Apollo, god of light and youth; Poseidon, god of the sea; Athena, goddess of war and wisdom; and Aphrodite, goddess of love and beauty. Many Greek myths and legends were written about their gods and goddesses.

The Greeks built many temples for their gods and goddesses. One of the most famous temples was the Parthenon, the temple of Athena. Today, parts of it still stand in Athens on a hill known as the Acropolis.

Each year, the Greeks celebrated festivals in honor of their gods. One festival gathered people from all over Greece for a contest of running and throwing. The festival was called the Olympic Games!

• Write a paragraph telling how life in Sparta and Athens differed. Tell which city you would have wanted to live in, and why.

Greece

Name_____

Underline.

The word **democracy** means. . .

    a way of life that encourages people to exercise.

    a way of life that allows people to take part in their own government.

Ancient Greece had two main cities: _____ _____
                                                     A   B

Write A or B.

____ Believed in developing the mind as well as the body

____ Emphasized physical activities

____ Young boys were trained in gymnastics and other sports.

____ Individuals were encouraged to develop their own talents.

____ Most citizens grew into strong adults.

____ They learned mathematics, literature, writing and music, as well as gymnastics.

____ Very few people could read or write.

____ The city became the center of Greek culture.

Check, write, circle.

The ancient Greeks

. . .built homes of ☐ stone and brick ☐ wood around open _____.

. . .worshipped ☐ many ☐ twelve gods.

. . .wore hoods / cloaks and sandals. / boots.

. . .ate only one / two meals a day, called: _____ and _____.
                                                          morning   night

Write.

Gods and Goddesses. . . Who were they?

_____ goddess of love and beauty

_____ ruler of all other gods and goddesses

_____ god of light and youth

_____ goddess of war and wisdom

_____ god of the sea

Zeus was believed to live on _____ _____.

The _____ was the temple of Athena.

The Parthenon still stands in the city of _____.

Think About:

Ancient Rome

Ancient Rome was a powerful civilization which began almost 3000 years ago.

No one knows exactly how Rome was founded. Legend says that twin brothers, Romulus and Remus, were the founders of Rome. The legend says that the twin boys were cast into the Tiber River as babies. They were saved by a she-wolf, who raised them. As young men, they built a city on the spot where the wolf had pulled them from the river. The city was Rome.

The lives of the ancient Romans centered around the forum, an open marketplace where public meetings were held. Many of the Roman rulers built their own forums. Today, ruins of these forums still stand, including the forum of the great Roman emperor, Julius Caesar.

The Romans lived in houses which consisted of one large four-sided room called an atrium. Wealthy Romans added many more rooms around their atriums. Some homes even had piped-in water.

The Ancient Romans ate three meals a day. Their breakfast was usually bread and honey. For lunch they ate meat and fruit. Dinner was their largest meal, often served as a banquet. It included eggs, fish, meat, vegetables and fruit. In place of butter, the Romans used olive oil. Instead of sugar, they used honey.

The Romans wore a garment called a tunica. A tunica had short sleeves and hung to the knees. Tunicas were worn by both men and women. The men wore a draped cloth, called a toga, over the tunica.

The Romans worshipped many gods, such as Juno, Mars and Jupiter. The Romans later adopted some of the Greek gods and goddesses and gave them new names. For example, the Greek goddess Aphrodite became the Roman goddess, Venus.

The ancient Romans were very interested in law and government. They established principles of law that are still used today. One principle was called equity. It meant that a law should be flexible enough to fit different circumstances.

The ancient Romans were famous for their many festivals which were usually held in the huge open theater called the Colosseum. There they watched gladiators either fight each other or wild beasts.

One of the most popular events was the chariot races held in a large arena called a circus. The largest circus in ancient Rome was called the Circus Maximus, which held 180,000 Roman spectators.

● Write an example of a situation today in which the principle of equity would be important.

10

Rome

Write 1-5.   How was Rome Founded?

Legend says...

○ Twin baby boys, Romulus and Remus, were cast into the Tiber River.

○ Romulus and Remus built a city on the spot where they were saved.

○ Romulus and Remus were raised by the she-wolf.

○ The city was called Rome.

○ The baby boys were pulled from the river by a she-wolf.

Underline, check.

The forum. . .

was a one room house that people lived in.
was an open marketplace where public meetings were held.

Many Roman rulers ☐ built their own forums. ☐ burned forums.

Circle, match, write.

The ancient Romans ate   four meals a day.
                         three

breakfast   meat and fruit
lunch   eggs, fish, meat, vegetables and fruit
dinner   bread and honey

In place of sugar, the Romans used _____.

In place of butter, the Romans used _____.

Check.

The Romans lived in one large four-sided room called:

☐ lodge   ☐ an atrium   ☐ a great room

True or False

The ancient Romans...

_____ adopted some of the Greek gods and goddesses.

_____ used the Greek names for their gods and goddesses.

_____ established principles of law.

_____ held festivals in the open theater called the Colosseum.

_____ watched chariot races in the forum.

_____ watched chariot races in an arena called a circus.

The largest circus in Rome was called the

_____, which held _ _ _, _ _ _ spectators.

Underline the sentence which explains the meaning of equity, a principle of law.

Think About:

The Decathlon

The decathlon is one of the most famous contests in sports. Decathlon is a Greek word which means "ten contests." The first decathlon was added to the Olympic Games in 1912. It was added in honor of athletes who competed in the original Olympic Games in Greece. Most of the games in the early Olympics were contests of running, jumping and throwing. Today, these kinds of events are called track and field events.

A decathlon is a two-day contest that features ten separate events in track and field. The events for the first day are the 100-meter dash, long jump, shot-put, high jump and the 400-meter run. The events for the second day are the 110-meter hurdles, discus throw, pole vault, javelin throw and the 1500-meter run.

The 100-meter dash starts the decathlon. It takes just seconds for the athletes to run the 100-meter race, which is approximately the length of a football field.

An athlete has three chances for a high score in the long jump and high jump events. The best score out of three attempts is used.

The shot-put is an event that requires a tremendous amount of power to throw a 16-pound metal ball, called a shot, as far as possible.

The final event of the first day is the 400-meter run. This race is almost a quarter of a mile in length. It is a hard race to run because it is too long to run in one burst of energy. But it is too short to run at a slower pace. Some people have called this the "murderous race."

The second day begins with the 110-meter hurdles. The runners must not only run fast, but also jump over ten hurdles which are 3½ feet tall.

The discus throw is an event in which an athlete throws a four-pound metal plate, called a discus, as far as possible.

The pole vault is one of the hardest events of the decathlon. An athlete runs and lifts himself high into the air on a pole. The aim is to jump over a high bar without knocking it down.

The javelin throw event requires an athlete to throw a javelin, a kind of spear, as far as possible.

The final event is the 1500-meter race, which is just a little less than a mile in distance.

The goal of every decathlon athlete is to win the gold medal in the Olympic games. The winner is often called "the world's greatest athlete."

• Find the names of three Olympic Decathlon winners.

12

The Decathlon   Name_____

The Decathlon...

_____ is one of the most famous contests in sports.

_____ is a Greek word that means "no contest."

_____ was added to the Olympic Games in 1912.   25 pts

_____ was added to the Olympic Games in honor of the Greek god, Zeus.

_____ was added to the Olympic games in honor of the athletes who competed in the original Olympic Games.

_____ is a Greek word that means "ten contests."

Write.

Name the five events for each day of the decathlon.

First day   ## Second Day

_____   _____

_____   _____

_____   _____

_____   _____

_____   _____

Write the name of the event (or events) by each sentence.

_____ An athlete throws a four-pound metal plate as far as possible.

_____ This race is approximately the length of a football field. It takes just seconds to run.

_____ An athlete jumps over a high bar by using a pole to lift himself into the air.

_____ An athlete has three chances for a high score.

_____ The final event of the second day. The race is a little less than a mile.

_____ An athlete throws a 16-pound metal ball as far as possible.

_____ While running, an athlete jumps over ten hurdles which are 3½ feet tall.

_____ An athlete throws a "spear" as far as possible.

_____ The final event of the first day. This race is called "the murderous race."

Think About:

The World Series

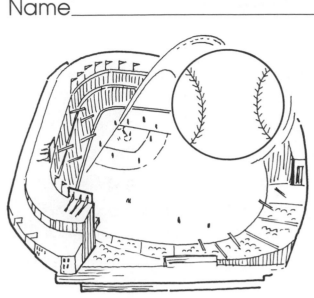

Every year baseball takes center stage for one of the world's most famous sporting events—the World Series. The World Series is a series of baseball games which decide the world championship of baseball.

The World Series matches the American League champion team against the National League champion team. The first team to win four games out of seven wins the World Series.

The World Series was first played in 1903. The American League champions, the Boston Pilgrims, played the National League champions, the Pittsburgh Pirates. This first World Series was won by the Boston Pilgrims, now named the Boston Red Sox.

Although the World Series seemed off to a great start in 1903, the next year was a different story. In 1904, the New York Giants refused to play the Boston Pilgrims in the World Series. To this day, no one is sure why they refused, but 1904 was to be the only year in World Series history which did not have a world championship series.

For a team to make it to the World Series takes months of hard work and a lot of talent. Most teams play over 150 games between April and October of each year. At the end of the regular season, the two best teams from each league play in the World Series.

Through the years, many great baseball players, such as Babe Ruth, Jackie Robinson, Joe Di Maggio and Lou Gehrig, have played in the World Series.

Some performances are hard to forget, such as Reggie Jackson's three straight home runs in the last game of the 1977 World Series.

Many World Series records have been broken through the years. But one record which has never been broken was set in 1956 by a little-known player named Don Larsen, who pitched a no-hitter game for the New York Yankees.

● Find the names of the last two teams to play in the World Series.

Write.

The _____ _____ decides the championship of baseball.

The World Series is played between the champions of the _____

League and _____ League.

14

The World Series

Name_____

Circle.
The first team to win   four / three   out of   eight / seven   games wins the World Series.

Write.
The first World Series was played in _____.
year

☐ The Boston Pilgrims were the _____ champions.

☐ The Pittsburgh Pirates were the _____ champions.

Put a ✓ in the box by the team which won the first World Series.

Circle.
Today, the Boston Pilgrims are named the Boston   Cardinals. / Red Sox.

True or False

_____ The World Series has been played every year since 1903.

_____ In 1904, the New York Giants refused to play the Boston Pilgrims.

_____ The New York Giants were sick with the flu and could not play.

_____ No one is sure why the Giants refused to play the Pilgrims.

_____ 1904 was the only year in World Series history which did not have a championship series.

Circle and write.
Most baseball teams play over   150 / 250   games between _____
month
and _____.
month

Underline.
In the first sentence of the story, the expression "takes centerstage" means. . .
    baseball is played on a field instead of a stage.
    baseball becomes the center of attention.

Write, circle.
In the 1977 World Series, _____
player's name

hit   3 / 5   straight _____ in the last game.

Write, underline.
In the 1956 World Series, _____ pitched
player's name
    a three-run game for the Yankees.
    a no-hitter game for the Yankees.

In the story, underline the names of great baseball players in World Series history.

Think About:

Stanley Cup

Name_____

Today, one of the most popular spectator sports in the world is ice hockey. Each year, the teams of the National Hockey League play a series of games to determine the championship of ice hockey. The winner is presented an award called the Stanley Cup. The Stanley Cup is one of the most prestigious awards in the world of sports.

Ice hockey is now an international sport. But nowhere is hockey more popular than in Canada. Over 125 years ago, hockey-on-ice was played in Montreal, Canada. In 1870, the first official rules of the game were written. By 1880, official teams were organized into leagues. Some of those first games were played on town ice rinks which had bandstands right in the middle of the rinks! Later, special ice hockey rinks were built which even featured lights hung from telegraph poles.

The popularity of the game seemed to sweep through Canada. One of hockey's greatest fans was Lord Stanley of Preston, the sixth Governor General of Canada. Lord Stanley organized a championship game in which Canadian ice hockey teams would compete. On March 22, 1894, the first Stanley Cup game was played in Montreal, Canada, at Victoria Rink. The championship game received its name from the award presented to the winner. Donated by Lord Stanley, the first award was a sterling silver cup.

After that first championship game in 1894, the game of ice hockey continued to grow in popularity. Today, the National Hockey League includes teams from America as well as Canada. And each year, the teams play a series of games to determine who wins the championship of ice hockey **and** the Stanley Cup.

● Find out how many teams in the National Hockey League are Canadian and how many are American.

Write.
The _____ is the award presented to the championship team in ice hockey.

Circle.
Ice hockey was played in Montreal, Canada / London, over 200 / 125 years ago.

The Stanley Cup

True or False.

Ice Hockey...

_____ is played each year in the Stanley Sports Center.

_____ teams of the National League play a series of games for the championship.

_____ is now an international sport.

_____ was probably first played in France.

_____ is probably most popular in Canada.

Underline.

Some of the first games...
    were played on indoor ice rinks in Montreal.
    were played on town ice rinks which had bandstands.
Later, special ice hockey rinks were built...
    which featured lights hung from telegraph poles.
    which were named after each hockey team.

Write.

One of ice hockey's greatest fans was _____ of Preston.

Check.

Lord Stanley was ☐ the mayor of Montreal, Canada.
                 ☐ the sixth Governor General of Canada.

Circle.

Lord Stanley organized a championship game in which American ice
                          charity   Canadian

hockey teams would compete.

Write.

When was the first Stanley Cup game played? _____, 18___

In what city was the first Stanley Cup game played?

_____, _____.

At what rink was the first Stanley Cup game played? _____.

Underline the sentence that tells how the Stanley Cup game got its name.

Check.

The word **prestigious** means: ☐ honored and important.
                                ☐ cautious and careful.

Think About:

Leonardo da Vinci

Leonardo da Vinci was one of the greatest artists of all time. He is remembered not only as a painter, but also as a sculptor, musician, inventor, astronomer, scientist and engineer.

Leonardo was born in 1452, in Vinci, Italy. As a young boy, he showed a talent for mathematics and painting. His father took him to Florence, Italy, to study painting and engineering. Florence was a city where many well-known artists lived. Leonardo became well-known in Florence as a gifted young painter. Soon he was painting better than his teachers. In 1472, at the age of twenty, Leonardo was asked to join the painter's guild in Florence. This was an honor for Leonardo to be officially accepted by so many other great artists.

When Leonardo was thirty years old, he decided to move to Milan, Italy. He began working for the Duke of Milan, who wanted to make Milan a beautiful and famous city like Florence.

While in Milan, Leonardo painted one of the most famous paintings in history—"The Last Supper."

"The Last Supper" was painted on the wall of a small church near the duke's castle. People came from many countries to see the painting. The King of France liked the painting so much that he wanted to move the

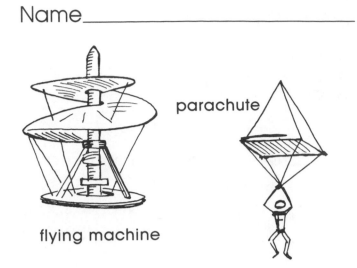

parachute

flying machine

entire church back to France. Today, the painting is still found on the wall of the little church in Italy.

In 1499, Leonardo returned to Florence. Here he painted his other famous painting, the "Mona Lisa." The "Mona Lisa" was a painting of a twenty-four year old wife of a wealthy merchant. Her name was Lisa del Gioconda. The painting is famous for Lisa's mysterious smile. For centuries, people have wondered what her smile really meant.

Leonardo is remembered for other contributions, such as sketch designs for flying machines long before anyone ever believed man could fly. Leonardo also drew detailed sketches of the human body and how it worked. He wrote thousands of pages of notes on mathematics and science. Sometimes he even wrote his notes backwards and read them with a mirror!

Many of Leonardo's sketches and notes have been used through the years to help scientists and inventors make new discoveries.

• Write your name and address backwards. Use a mirror to read them.

Leonardo da Vinci

Name_____

Write.

Leonardo is remembered not only as a painter, but also a:

_____   _____   _____

_____   _____   _____

True or False

_____ As a young boy, Leonardo showed a talent for mathematics and painting.

_____ Leonardo's father took him to Rome, Italy, to study painting and engineering.

_____ Florence was a city where many well-known artists lived.

_____ Leonardo became well-known in Florence as a gifted young painter.

_____ Leonardo became dissatisfied and stopped painting.

_____ Leonardo was soon painting better than his teachers.

_____ In 1472, Leonardo was asked to join the painter's guild in Florence.

Write.

When Leonardo was thirty, he moved to _____, Italy.

Write and underline.

There he worked for the _____ of _____, who wanted to. . .

    make Leonardo a famous painter.

    make Milan a beautiful and famous city like Florence.

While in Milan, Leonardo painted one of the most famous paintings in history, called _____.

Check, circle, write.

"The Last Supper". . .

☐ was painted on the wall of a small church.

☐ was so famous that people came from other countries to see it.

☐ was moved to Rome, Italy, in 1650.

☐ is still found on the wall of the little church in Italy.

In 1499, Leonardo returned to   Florence.
    Vienna.

In Florence, he painted a portrait of the wife of a wealthy merchant. The painting is called the _____. The lady in the painting was named _____ .

The painting is famous for: ☐ its unusual colors.
  ☐ Lisa's mysterious smile.

Raphael

Raphael was one of the greatest artists in history. He was born in Urbino, Italy, in 1483. Raphael's father was a painter. He encouraged Raphael to begin painting at an early age. As a young man, Raphael was sent to study with Peruginoi, a master painter of the day. Peruginoi became a great influence on Raphael's style of painting. Before long, he was painting better than his teacher.

Raphael's work attracted the attention of a wealthy merchant, Angelo Doni, who hired Raphael to paint for him. He painted many portraits and religious scenes. These paintings made him wealthy.

In 1504, Raphael traveled to Florence, where he studied painting for four years. It was during this time that he painted "The Entombment," one of his most famous paintings. It was also during this time that he painted many of the Madonnas, for which he is so famous.

In 1508, Raphael returned to Urbino. He was hired to paint for the Duke of Urbino. The duke asked for a group of paintings that told the story of St. George. St. George was a legendary hero who lived in ancient times. According to the legend, St. George slew a terrible dragon and saved the King's daughter. These paintings made Raphael even more respected as an artist.

This same year, Raphael left for Rome. At the same time, Michelangelo, another great painter in Rome, was painting the ceiling of the Sistine Chapel.

During this time in Rome, Raphael painted the masterpieces for which he is most famous. He became so popular that he could hardly finish all the work he was hired to do. Whenever he left his house, he was surrounded by admirers. Young painters followed him hoping to learn from him. He was called the "Divine Raphael." Raphael's last great work, the "Transfiguration" was completed by one of his pupils.

In 1514, Raphael was made chief architect of St. Paul's Church in Rome. He painted many beautiful madonnas during this time.

In 1520, Raphael became ill and died. His death saddened all of Rome.

• Find out more about the legendary St. George. Write a story of his adventure.

Raphael...

_____ was one of the greatest artists in history.

_____ was born in Urbino, Italy, in 1483.

_____ was the son of a doctor.

_____ was encouraged by his father to begin painting at an early age.

_____ was sent to study painting with Michelangelo.

_____ was sent to study painting with Peruginoi.

_____ became a better painter than his teacher.

Write, circle.

A wealthy merchant, _____, hired Raphael to paint for him.

Raphael's paintings made him   wealthy.
                                unhappy.

In 1504, Raphael moved to _____, where he studied painting

for   ten   years.
       four

Write.

During this time . . .

    Raphael painted his famous painting, _____.

    Raphael painted many of the _____, for which he is so famous.

In 1508, Raphael returned to _____, where he was hired to paint for

   the _____ of _____.

The duke asked Raphael for a group of paintings that told the story

   of St. _____.

Underline.

St. George . . .

    was a legendary hero who lived in ancient times.

    was the King of Urbino who lived in ancient times.

Check.

While in Rome . . .

☐ Raphael painted many masterpieces.

☐ Raphael became extremely popular as a painter.

☐ Raphael painted the ceiling of the Sistine Chapel.

Write.

Raphael was called the "_____."

Think About:

Rembrandt

Rembrandt was one of the greatest artists of all time. He was born on July 15, 1606, in Leiden, Holland. Rembrandt began painting at an early age. At the age of fifteen, he traveled to Amsterdam to study art. But he soon returned home to paint on his own.

Rembrandt's first paintings were of subjects from the Bible and from history. He used bright colors and glossy paints. These paintings were very popular, and soon, Rembrandt was well-known in his community.

In 1628, Rembrandt began to teach art. He was a respected teacher with many students.

In 1632, Rembrandt again moved to Amsterdam. He began painting portraits of many well-known people in Amsterdam. He soon became famous in Holland for his beautiful portraits.

In 1634, he married a wealthy and educated girl named Saskia. They moved into a large home where Rembrandt hung many of the paintings that he had collected.

Rembrandt continued to succeed as an artist. But tragedy began to strike his family. Three of his four children died at a very early age. And then in 1642, his wife, Saskia, died.

Rembrandt became very sad. He began to paint with darker colors. But, somehow, his painting grew even more beautiful. He used dark colors around the figures in his paintings. The figures themselves were painted as if a soft light were shining on them.

Rembrandt began to paint more for himself and less for other people. Although his work was brilliant, he was not able to make enough money to keep his house. In 1657, his house and his possessions were auctioned off. Rembrandt was bankrupt.

But until he died on October 4, 1669, Rembrandt continued to paint. His most famous painting was named "The Night Watch."

Rembrandt created over 600 paintings, 300 etchings and 1400 drawings. Some of his most fascinating paintings were the portraits which he painted of himself. The hundred self-portraits leave a remarkable record of his lifetime.

● Draw a self-portrait.

Check.

Rembrandt's first paintings were of subjects from the

[ ] legends   and from   [ ] history.
[ ] Bible   [ ] myths.

True or False

Rembrandt ...

_____ was one of the greatest artists of all time.

_____ was born on July 15, 1606, in Florence, Italy.

_____ began painting at an early age.

_____ traveled to Amsterdam at the age of fifteen to study art.

_____ stayed in Amsterdam for thirteen years.

Check and write.

Rembrandt used [ ] soft [ ] bright colors and _____ paints.

Underline.

In 1634, Rembrandt married . . .
   a wealthy and educated girl named Saskia.
   a poor girl from Amsterdam named Saskia.

Check, write.

Although Rembrandt was successful as an artist,

[ ] tragedy [ ] good fortune   began to strike his family.

Three of his _____ children died at a very early age.

In 1642, [ ] Rembrandt's father died.
          [ ] Rembrandt's wife died.

Rembrandt's sadness caused him to use [ ] darker [ ] lighter colors.

Underline.

In 1657 . . .
   Rembrandt sold his house and moved to Italy.
   Rembrandt's house and possessions were auctioned off.

Check, circle, write.

Rembrandt was [ ] bankrupt.   [ ] retired.

Rembrandt died on October 4, 1669.
                              1700.

Rembrandt's more famous painting was named _____ .

Rembrandt's other works included:
   [ ] paintings   [ ] drawings
   [ ] etchings   [ ] self-portraits

Underline the sentences which describe how Rembrandt used dark and light colors to help "spotlight" the figure he was painting.

Think About:

Vincent Van Gogh

Vincent Van Gogh is remembered as one of the greatest painters of modern art. It is hard to believe that the life of one of the world's most famous painters was filled with so much loneliness and disappointment.

Vincent Van Gogh was born in Zundert, Holland, in 1853. Most of his young manhood was spent trying to find a suitable career that he could succeed in. At the age of sixteen, he left home to live with an uncle who was an art dealer. Vincent was not successful, and he soon left. He had not enjoyed being a businessman. He wanted to be a minister.

At the age of twenty-five, Van Gogh became a preacher in a poor mining town in Belgium. He was so concerned for the poor that he went without food so that he could give more to the poor. But some church officials did not approve of Vincent's behavior. He was released from his duties as a minister.

By 1880, Van Gogh had decided to become a painter. In his early years as a painter, he completed "The Potato Eaters," one of his finest paintings. He chose dark gray and brown colors to paint the poor Dutch peasants eating dinner after working hard through the day.

In 1886, Van Gogh moved to Paris to be near his brother, Theo, who was a great admirer of Van Gogh's work.

In 1888, Van Gogh moved once again. This time he traveled to Arles in France. It was here that Van Gogh's style of painting began to change. Before, he had used many dark, even drab colors in his painting. But now, he began painting with bright, intense colors, such as red and yellow. His painting, "Sunflowers," was an example of how his work had changed. Van Gogh also began using a flat knife, instead of a brush, to apply thick paint in heavy strokes.

Van Gogh was painting more than he had ever painted before. In the last five years of his life, he painted more than *eight hundred* paintings! Many painters have not completed that many paintings in a lifetime!

But Van Gogh was becoming a troubled man. He also began suffering from seizures. During one seizure, he cut off his ear. Van Gogh died in July, 1890.

Van Gogh sold only one painting during his lifetime. He received no praise for his work. Only after his death was his work recognized for its greatness. One of the greatest painters of all time died thinking that he was a failure!

• Fine the names of three more famous paintings by Van Gogh.

Vincent Van Gogh

Name_____

Check.

Vincent Van Gogh . . .

☐ is remembered as one of the greatest painters of modern art.

☐ had a life filled with much loneliness and disappointment.

☐ had a life filled with excitement and adventure.

Circle, write.

Vincent Van Gogh was born in 1753, in _____, Holland.
1853,

At the age of twenty-five, Van Gogh became a _____ in a poor

mining town in Italy.
Belgium.

Circle, write, check.

By 1880, Van Gogh had decided to become a teacher.
painter.

One of his finest paintings, _____, showed Dutch
peasants eating dinner after working hard through the day.

He painted with dark yellow and brown colors.
gray   green

In 1888, Van Gogh moved to Arles, _____.

Van Gogh's style of painting ☐ began to change.
☐ stayed the same.

He began painting with ☐ dull ☐ bright and intense colors, such as _____
and yellow.

An example of his new style was the painting, _____.

Van Gogh painted with a ☐ brush. ☐ flat knife.

Check, write, circle.

Van Gogh

. . . began to suffer from ☐ seizures. ☐ tuberculosis.

. . . painted more than _____ paintings in the

last ten years of his life.
five

. . . sold ☐ only eight ☐ only one painting during his lifetime.

. . . received ☐ no praise ☐ much praise for his work during his lifetime.

. . . died in July, _____.

. . . died thinking he was a _____.

Think About:

Johann Sebastian Bach

Johann Sebastian Bach is known as one of the greatest musicians of all time. Bach was born on March 21, 1685, in Germany. Bach's family was famous in Germany because of their music. Many of Bach's aunts, uncles, cousins, brothers and sisters sang or played musical instruments. Bach's father taught him to play the violin at an early age.

When Bach was only ten years old, his mother and father died. Bach went to live with an older brother. Bach's brother taught him to play the harpsichord and the clavichord, which were forerunners of the piano.

Bach also began to play the organ. This became his favorite instrument. Sometimes he would walk over a hundred miles to hear the music of Remken, the greatest organist of the time.

Bach was becoming more and more interested in music. He began composing music. He became famous as an organist and a composer.

One day he was asked to compete in a harpsichord contest. The contest was held in the court of King Ferdinand Augustus. Bach was to compete with a famous French musician, named Marchand. On the day of the contest, Marchand left Germany. Many said he was afraid to perform with the great Bach. Bach played so well that he was asked to

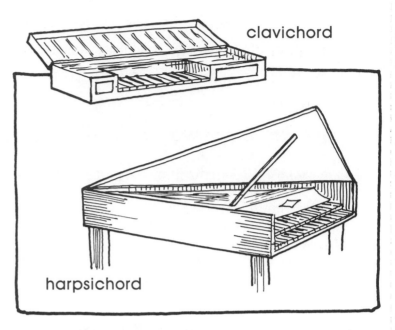

clavichord

harpsichord

stay as a court musician.

By this time, Bach was married and had seven children. But in 1720, his wife, Maria, died. Bach later married again and had thirteen more children.

Bach spent his later years as a director of music for a large school. Here, he continued to compose music. His compositions were famous for their style, called baroque.

Baroque music is lively—it is played in constant motion. Today, Bach is called the "genius of baroque music."

Bach's twenty children became musicians. Two sons, C.P.E. Bach and Johann Christian Bach became well-known as composers. But neither became as famous as their father, Johann Sebastian Bach, who is remembered today as "The Father of Modern Music."

• Write about Bach's children that became famous composers.

Circle, write, check.

Johann Sebastian **Bach**

. . .was one of the greatest   musicians / artists   of all time.

. . .was born on March 21, 1685, in _____.

. . .was born into a family of well-known   artists. / musicians.

. . .was taught to play the ☐ piano ☐ violin by his father.

. . .was _____ years old when his parents died.
After the death of his parents, Bach went to live
☐ with his grandparents. ☐ by himself. ☐ with an older brother.

Write.
Bach's brother taught him to play the _____ and

   the _____.
Both instruments were forerunners of the _____.

Check.
Bach also began to play the ☐ organ. ☐ french horn.

Underline.
Sometimes Bach. . .
   would perform for the great organist, Remken.
   would walk over a hundred miles to hear the great organist, Remken.

Check.
Soon, Bach became famous as. . .
☐ a teacher.   ☐ a composer.
☐ an organist.   ☐ an author.

Circle, write, check.

Bach was asked to compete in a   harpsicord / organ   contest, held in the court of

   King _____.

Bach was to compete with the famous ☐ German ☐ French   musician,

   named _____.

On the day of the contest,   Bach / Marchand   left Germany.

Underline.
Many said that Marchand. . .
   was ill and unable to perform in the contest.
   was afraid to perform with the great Bach.

Write.
Bach played so well that he was asked to stay as a _____.

Think About:

Wolfgang Amadeus Mozart

Wolfgang Amadeus Mozart was known as the "Wonder Child," who later became one of the greatest composers of all time.

Mozart was born on January 27, 1756, in Austria. When he was just three years old, he learned to play the harpsicord. By the time he was five years old, he was composing music. At the age of six, he was invited to perform for the Empress of Austria. Mozart astonished people with his musical ability. He was called a child genius.

Mozart's father, Leopold, was a well-known musician. He was very proud of his son. Leopold took Mozart on tours through Europe. Mozart performed for kings and queens, other musicians and in churches.

In 1781, Mozart left his home town and traveled to Vienna, Austria. He married the next year. Mozart did not have a regular job. He earned a living by selling the music which he wrote. He also gave music lessons and performed his music in public.

Mozart continued to compose music. His compositions included operas, symphonies, concertos, serenades and church music.

Mozart wrote twenty-two operas. Today many of his operas are still famous, such as: "The Marriage of Figaro," "Don Giovanni"and"The Magic Flute."The first two are written in Italian. The last is written in German. Today, "Don Giovanni" is considered the world's greatest opera!

Mozart wrote at least forty symphonies for orchestras. His most famous symphony is nicknamed "The Jupiter."

He wrote special music for orchestras, called serenades. A serenade was a softer, lighter kind of music. Many serenades were written to be performed outdoors. One of his most famous serenades is called "A Little Night Music."

Mozart also composed music to be played with the orchestra playing in the background. Sometimes Mozart would perform these solos himself.

Mozart wrote many compositions for churches. His most famous work is called "Requiem." "Requiem" was a mass, or prayers, for the dead. He wrote part of "Requiem" while he was dying of an illness.

Mozart was only thirty-five years old when he died. He died a poor man on December 5, 1791.

Today, Mozart is considered to have been a musical genius. His music is known throughout the world.

• Find and write the story of the opera, "Don Giovanni."

Wolfgang Amadeus Mozart

Name_____

Write.

Wolfgang Amadeus Mozart was known as the "_____."

Circle and write.

Mozart was born on January 27, 1756, in _____.
 1854,

Match.

three years old	Mozart began composing music.
five years old	Mozart performed for the Empress of Austria.
six years old	Mozart learned to play the harpsicord.

True or False

_____ Mozart was called a child genius.

_____ Mozart's father, Leopold, was a well-known artist.

_____ Leopold took Mozart on tours through Europe.

_____ Mozart performed for kings and queens.

_____ In 1781, Mozart left home and traveled to England.

_____ In Vienna, Mozart made a living by selling his music and giving music lessons.

_____ Mozart married the year after moving to Vienna.

Write, circle.

Mozart's compositions included: _____, _____, _____,

_____ and _____.

Mozart wrote 12 operas. Three of his most famous operas are:
 22

_____   _____

_____

Put an X beside the opera considered to be the world's greatest opera.

Circle, write, check.

Mozart wrote at least four symphonies for _____.
 forty

His most famous symphony is nicknamed the _____.

Mozart wrote special music for orchestras called operas.
 serenades.

A serenade was a ☐ softer
☐ faster music written to be performed _____.
☐ lighter

One of Mozart's most famous serenades is called: _____.

Think About:

Frederic Chopin

Frederic Chopin was one of the most brilliant composers for piano in history. During his life, Chopin wrote over 200 compositions for piano.

Chopin was born on February 22, 1810, in Warsaw, Poland. He began to take piano lessons at age six. By the time he was eight, he was performing in public. At the age of twelve, he was composing his own music. Chopin was considered to be a child prodigy—a child with an extraordinary talent.

For several years, Chopin traveled through the country performing his music. At one concert, the Czar of Russia was so thrilled with Chopin's music that he gave him a diamond and gold ring. Although Chopin enjoyed performing for large groups, he preferred playing for small groups in the homes of friends.

When Chopin was twenty years old, he left Poland and moved to Paris, France. When he left his home, friends gave him a silver goblet filled with Polish earth. Chopin kept this gift for the rest of his life.

Chopin's music was very popular in Paris. He became a well-known music teacher. It was while living in Paris that Chopin met two very important people in his life. One was Franz Liszt, another famous composer. Liszt and Chopin became friends and

shared their love of music.

It was Liszt who introduced Chopin to a woman named George Sand, a French writer. Sand and Chopin became dear friends. Many of his most famous compositions were inspired by their friendship.

In 1839, Chopin became ill with tuberculosis. Although he traveled to an island near Spain to rest, his condition worsened. Chopin somehow managed to continue to compose and perform his music for several years.

On October 17, 1849, Chopin died at the age of 39. Chopin's own music was played at his funeral. The Polish earth, which Chopin had brought from Poland almost twenty years before, was sprinkled on his grave.

• Find the names of three of Chopin's compositions.

Underline.
Frederic Chopin. . .
    was one of the most brilliant composers for violin in history.
    was one of the most brilliant composers for piano in history.

30

Frederic Chopin

Circle and write.

Chopin wrote over
 500
 200
compositions for _____.

Chopin was born in
 1810
 1910
in Warsaw, _____.

Write.

Chopin was considered to be a child _____.

Check.

The term "child prodigy" means:

☐ a child who likes music.

☐ a child with an extraordinary talent.

Write, circle, match.

At the age of twenty, Chopin left _____ and moved to _____.

Friends gave Chopin a _____ goblet filled with _____ earth.

In Paris, Chopin became well-known as a
 lecturer.
 music teacher.

In Paris, Chopin met:

| Franz Liszt | a French writer |
| George Sand | a famous composer |

Many of Chopin's compositions were inspired by his friendship

with _____.

Underline the sentence which tells what the Czar of Russia gave Chopin after his performance.

True or False

Chopin...

_____ became ill with tuberculosis in 1939.

_____ traveled to an island near Spain to rest.

_____ recovered and remained in good health for years.

_____ continued to compose for several years even though he was ill.

On October 17,
 1849,
 1900,
Chopin died at the age of _____.

Think About:

Peter Tchaikovsky

Peter Tchaikovsky composed some of the most beautiful music ever written for orchestras.

Tchaikovsky was born in Russia on May 7, 1840. His father and mother began piano lessons for him at an early age.

When Tchaikovsky was eleven, he was sent to a special school to study law. For several years he did not have time to think about his music. But at the age of twenty-two, he once again began to study music at the St. Petersburg Conservatory. Four years later, he became a teacher at the Moscow Conservatory of Music.

While teaching, Tchaikovsky began to compose. But with his teaching duties, it was hard to find the time he needed to write music. An important event took place which solved this problem. A rich admirer gave Tchaikovsky enough money to quit his teaching job and spend all his time writing music. Tchaikovsky never met this admirer in person, but they exchanged letters for years.

Over the next fourteen years, until his death on November 6, 1893, Tchaikovsky wrote some of the most beautiful compositions ever written.

Tchaikovsky wrote beautiful symphonies, concertos and operas. But his best known work may be his

three ballets: "Swan Lake," "Sleeping Beauty" and the "Nutcracker."

The "Nutcracker" tells the story of a little girl's dream. On Christmas night, she dreams that one of her gifts, a nutcracker, comes to life and battles an army of soldiers led by the Mouse King. In her dream, the nutcracker turns into a prince and carries her off to the Sugar Plum Kingdom. The ballet features a Russian Dance, Chinese Dance, Arab Dance, Dance of the Flutes and the Waltz of the Flowers.

Many of the melodies from the "Nutcracker," "Swan Lake" and other works are well-known today. That is why Tchaikovsky is often called the "Master of the Medley."

Tchaikovsky traveled to many countries, including America. In 1891, he went to New York City to take part in the opening of Carnegie Hall.

• Find and write the story of the ballet, "Swan Lake."

Underline.

Peter Tchaikovsky...

composed some of the most beautiful music ever written for orchestras.
composed some of the most beautiful music ever written for the organ.

Peter Tchaikovsky

Name_____

Write, circle, check.

Tchaikovsky was born in _____ on May 7, 1940.
1840.

His father and mother began ☐ violin ☐ piano lessons for him at an
early age.

When Tchaikovsky was eleven, he was sent to a special school to

study _____.

At the age of twenty-two, Tchaikovsky began to study law
music

at the _____.

Four years later, Tchaikovsky became a teacher at the _____

_____ of _____.

True or False

_____ While teaching, Tchaikovsky began to compose music.

_____ Tchaikovsky had plenty of time for composing his music.

_____ It was difficult for Tchaikovsky to find time for composing.

_____ A rich admirer gave Tchaikovsky money to quit teaching and spend his
time composing music.

_____ Tchaikovsky met his admirer only once.

_____ Tchaikovsky never met his admirer in person, but they exchanged
letters for years.

Circle and write.

Tchaikovsky's best known work may be his three waltzes:
ballets:

_____, _____ and the _____.

Underline.

The **Nutcracker** tells the story of. . .
a little girl's trip to the magic Christmas Village.
a little girl's dream on Christmas night.

Write, check, circle.

The little girl dreams that one of her gifts, a _____,

☐ comes to life and battles an army of soldiers.

☐ comes to life and teaches her to waltz.

The soldiers are led by the _____.

The nutcracker turns into a king and carries her off to the
prince

_____ Kingdom.

Think About:

The Typewriter

It might truly be said that the typewriter was one small invention that made a big difference. To understand how big the difference was, try to imagine what it was like when businesses had to write everything by hand. Every letter, every report, every bill, every memo—all had to be written by hand.

In the early 1800's, many inventors tried to make a machine that would take the place of so much handwriting. In 1867, an American, Christopher Sholes, decided to build a writing machine. His first experimental machine printed one letter—W. Sholes began working with two other inventors, Carlos Gliddon and Samuel Soule. In 1868, these three men designed the first typewriter. Their invention had 11 keys which typed only capital letters. Sholes continued to improve the invention. In 1874, a company put the typewriter on the market. Soon, other companies were producing typewriters. By the early 1900's, portable typewriters were being sold. In the 1920's, electric typewriters were on the market.

Today, there are 3 basic kinds of typewriters: standard, electric and automatic.

A standard typewriter works by power of the typist's hands. An electric typewriter is powered by electricity. Although the typist must still press the keys, the operation is much easier and faster than the standard typewriter.

An automatic typewriter has an electric typewriter keyboard connected to a computer. Together, the typewriter and the computer are called a word-processor. When a typist types on the keyboard, the computer stores the information. Then, the typewriter automatically types copies of the information.

Typewriters are made in several thousands of keyboard styles. Many electric typewriters have the letters and symbols on a ball which can be easily removed to change the style of type.

Special typewriters have letters and symbols in different languages. A typewriter called a wordwriter can type entire words, or even phrases, with a single touch of a key. Today, typewriters are continuing to change and advance with the Computer Age.

• Write a list of the ways you will use a typewriter in your future.

The Typewriter

True or False

_____ Before the typewriter, businesses had to write everything by hand.

_____ Before the typewriter, some businesses used word-processors.

_____ In the early 1800's, many inventors tried to make a writing machine.

_____ In 1867, Christopher Sholes decided to build a writing machine.

_____ Sholes first machine printed four letters—A, W, S, E.

_____ Sholes began to work with two other inventors.

_____ In 1868, the three men made a typewriter with 11 keys.

_____ Sholes became discouraged and quit.

_____ In 1874, a company put the typewriter on the market for sale.

Write, circle.

Name the three men who built the first working typewriter in 1868.

_____   _____

_____

Today, there are   three / five   basic kinds of typewriters:

1. _____   2. _____   3. _____

Check.

A standard typewriter

☐ works by the power of the typist's hands.
☐ is powered by a computer.
☐ is powered by a word-processor.
☐ is powered by electricity.

An electric typewriter

Write.

Together, the typewriter and computer are called a _____.

Write 1, 2, 3.

How does a word processor work?

◯ The typewriter automatically types copies of the information.

◯ A typist types information on the keyboard.

◯ The computer stores the information.

Check, write.

Some typewriters have letters and symbols . . .

☐ in the computer.   ☐ in special languages.

A typewriter, called a _____, can type words or phrases.

Underline the sentence that tells some of the things that businesses had to do by hand before the invention of the typewriter.

Think About:
The Telescope

The invention of the telescope opened up outer space for observation and study. Before the telescope, people could only guess about the stars, planets and other heavenly bodies. The only knowledge of space was gathered by what people could see with the naked eye. With the invention of the telescope, it was possible to discover, study and even photograph outer space.

Many people believe that the telescope was invented by Galileo, the great Italian astronomer. But most historians believe that a Dutch optician, named Hans Lippershey, made the first telescope in 1608. He was not allowed to have a patent for his invention.

Galileo heard of Lippershey's invention and the following year, 1609, he built his own telescope. Galileo's telescope magnified heavenly bodies 33 times larger than they appear to the naked eye. Galileo made some amazing discoveries with his telescope. He discovered the rings around the planet Saturn. He discovered that the moon has mountains and valleys; until then the moon was believed to have a smooth surface. Perhaps Galileo's greatest discovery was that four moons orbit the planet Jupiter. He called these moons the Medician stars. The name came from the Medici family which ruled Galileo's home province in Italy.

Galileo's discoveries created a sensation. He became famous, but many people were also suspicious and frightened by his discoveries.

Today, discoveries in space are still being made almost daily using telescopes of much greater strength.

One of the simplest kinds of telescopes is the refracting telescope, made with a long tube. One end of the tube contains two lenses called the eyepiece and ocular. They are used to magnify the image to be seen. The other end of the tube contains the objective lens, which gathers the light from the object to be seen. When light rays strike the objective lens, they bend and gather at one spot called the focal point. The eyepiece takes the light rays, or image, at the focal point and magnifies that image.

Another kind of telescope is called the reflecting telescope. Sir Issac Newton built one of the first reflecting telescopes. Instead of glass lenses in the objective, it uses mirrors. The reflecting telescope is used to see objects that are at greater distances because it can gather more light than a refracting telescope.

There are other more advanced telescopes being developed today. Because of telescopes, the science of astronomy is possible. With new and better telescopes, we will learn even more about our universe.

• Draw a picture showing the discoveries which were made by Galileo through his telescope.

The Telescope

Name_____

Check.

Before the telescope, people. . .

☐ could only guess about many of the stars and planets.

☐ thought that there were rings around the moon.

☐ gained their knowledge of space by what could be seen with the naked eye.

The term "naked eye" means. . .

☐ seeing something for the first time.

☐ seeing without the aid of magnification.

True or False

_____ Lippershey was not allowed to have a patent for his invention.

_____ Galileo built his own telescope in 1609.

_____ Galileo built the first telescope in history.

_____ Galileo's telescope magnified heavenly bodies 33 times.

_____ Galileo was unable to discover anything new in space.

What were Galileo's amazing discoveries?

_____

_____

Write.

Name two kinds of telescopes:

_____   _____
          A   B

Write A, B.

_____ Sir Issac Newton built one of the first ones.

_____ One of the simplest kinds of telescopes

_____ Uses a mirror in the objective, instead of glass

_____ Bends light rays to form a focal point

_____ Used to see objects that are at a greater distance

Write 1, 2, 3, 4.

How does a refracting telescope work?

____ The objective lens bends the light rays.

____ The eyepiece takes the light rays at the focal point and magnifies that image.

____ The objective lens gathers light from the object to be seen.

____ The bent light rays form a focal point.

Think About:

The Hot-Air Balloon

For thousands of years, people have been fascinated with the idea of flying. The idea was especially appealing to two French brothers, Jacques and Joseph Montgolfier. In the late 1700's, they began experimenting with the idea of a hot-air balloon.

Their first experiment was to fill small paper bags with smoke. They found that the bags would rise in the air. The Montgolfiers first believed that the smoke made the bags rise. But later, they realized that it was the hot air, and not the smoke itself, that caused the bags to rise.

The Montgolfier brothers continued to experiment. In 1783, they put a hot-air balloon in the air for eight minutes. The balloon carried a rooster, a sheep and a duck! They landed safely after history's first real balloon flight.

The next month, a French scientist, Jean de Rozier, became the first person to fly in a hot-air balloon. The balloon was made by the Montgolfier brothers. The balloon rose over 300 feet into the air. The flight lasted 25 minutes as de Rozier floated over Paris, France.

About the same time that the Montgolfier brothers were making their hot-air balloons, another Frenchman, named Jacques Charles, was making a balloon that was filled with hydrogen, a gas which is lighter than air.

In December of 1783, Charles made the first flight in a hydrogen balloon. His balloon rose over 2000 feet into the air. He flew 25 miles from where he started.

In the next year, ballooning became very popular in France. People traveled for miles to see balloons take off and land. Many of the balloonists became heroes.

On January 7, 1785, two men made the first balloon flight across the English Channel. The flight from England to France took two hours.

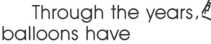

Through the years, balloons have been used for sport. But since their invention, balloons have been used for more serious purposes, too.

In the 1700's and 1800's, balloons were used in wars to observe the enemy troops. In 1863, Thaddeus Lowe, an American balloonist, directed an entire balloon corps which flew for the Union Army. Balloons were also used in World War I and World War II.

Today, hot-air balloons are made of nylon or polyester. To fly a balloon, the pilot burns fuel to produce hot air which inflates the balloon. The balloon rises in the air as more hot air is produced. To lower the balloon, hot air is released.

• Find the names of the men who first crossed the Atlantic Ocean in a hot-air balloon.

38

Hot-Air Balloons

Name_____

Underline.

For thousands of years . . .

    people have used hot-air balloons to fly across the country.

    people have been fascinated with the idea of flying.

Write, check, circle.

Two French brothers, _____ and _____ _____,

    began ☐ experimenting with the idea of a hot-air balloon.

          ☐ flying hot-air balloons for the French government.

For their first experiment, the brothers filled _____

with ☐ water. The smoke caused the bags to rise in the air.

       ☐ smoke.   hot air

True or False

_____ In 1783, the Montgolfier brothers put a hot-air balloon in the air.

_____ This first flight lasted eight minutes.

_____ The balloon carried a dog, mule and duck.

_____ Jean de Rozier was the first person to ride in a hot-air balloon.

_____ His flight lasted 25 minutes as he floated over Paris.

_____ The Montgolfiers' balloons were filled with hydrogen.

_____ Jacques Charles made a balloon filled with hydrogen.

_____ In 1783, Charles made the first flight in a hydrogen balloon.

Check, write, circle.

The word **hydrogen** means: ☐ air that is extremely hot.

                      ☐ a gas that is lighter than air.

Ballooning became very popular in ☐ Italy. ☐ France.

Many of the balloonists were treated as _____.

On January 7, 1785, two men made the first flight across the

_____.

The flight from _____ to _____ took two hours.

                                  twelve

Through the years, balloons have been used . . .

  ☐ for sport.

  ☐ to carry people to work each day.

  ☐ in wars to observe enemy troops.

In 1863, _____, an American balloonist, directed an

    entire balloon corps for the Union Army.

Think About:
The Television

The invention of the television changed the world in many important ways. Television has given people the opportunity to see and hear people, places and events from around the world. Television has become one of the world's most important forms of communication. The word "television" comes from the Greek word "tele," which means far, and the Latin word "videre," which means to see. Together, the words mean-**to see far.**

Television does not have just one inventor. In the 1800's, an Italian inventor named Marconi discovered how to send signals through the air as electromagnetic waves. His invention was the radio. This set the stage for the invention of television. In the early 1900's, a young American, Philo Farnsworth, began experimenting with an idea to send pictures as well as sound through the air. This idea resulted in the invention of the electronic television camera.

About the same time, an American scientist, Vladimir Zworykin, invented the iconoscope and the kinescope. The iconoscope was a television camera. The kinescope was a picture tube to receive and show the picture. In 1929, Zworykin made the first television system.

It wasn't until 1936 that regular broadcasts were made on television.

But how does a television work? The picture that you see on a television set comes from 3 basic steps. First, light and sound waves are changed into electronic signals. The light and sound waves come from the scene that is being televised. Next, these electronic signals are passed through the air to be received by individual television sets. Last, these signals are unscrambled and changed back into copies of the original light and sound waves to be seen and heard on a television set. In this way a picture is "moved" from the original scene to your television set.

These three steps can happen because it is possible to change light and sound waves into electronic signals. The light waves are picked up and changed into electronic signals by a camera. The sound waves are picked up and changed into electronic signals by a microphone. The camera signals are called video; the microphone signals are called audio.

To produce the electronic signals in color, certain color signals are added to the video. Three primary colors of light, red, blue and green, are used to produce television pictures in color.

Most electronic signals are carried through the air. Other means, such as microwaves, cable and satellites are also used to carry television signals.

• Write a paragraph telling how television can be used to educate people.

The Television

Name_____

Write.

The name television comes from:

the Greek word ① _____, which means _____ ②;

and the Latin word _____ ③, which means _____ _____ ④.

Together, the words mean _____ ⑤

True or False

_____ Television has only one inventor. ⑥

_____ In the 1800's, Marconi invented the television. ⑦

_____ Marconi learned how to send signals through the air as ⑧ electromagnetic waves. His invention was called radio.

_____ In the early 1900's, Philo Farnsworth invented the electronic television ⑨ camera.

_____ Vladimir Zworykin invented the iconoscope and the kinescope. ⑩

Write.

In 1929, _____ made the first television system. ⑪

Match.

iconoscope   a television camera ⑫

kinescope   a picture tube to receive the picture ⑬

Circle.

In   1958, ⑭
        1936, ⟩ regular broadcasts were made on television.

Write 1, 2, 3. ⟶ 1 = first   2 = Second   3 = third

How does a television work?

◯ The electronic signals are passed through the air to be received by ⑮ television sets.

◯ The signals are changed back to copies of original light and sound ⑯ waves.

◯ Light and sound waves are changed into electronic signals. ⑰

Write, check.

These three steps can happen because it is possible to change

_____ and _____ waves into electronic signals. ⑱ ⑲

Light waves are picked up and changed into electronic signals by

a _____ ⑳. The camera signals are called ☐ audio. ☐ video. ㉑

Sound waves are picked up and changed into electronic signals by

_____ ㉒. The microphone signals are called ☐ audio. ☐ video ㉓

To produce electronic signals in color, three _____ ㉔ colors of light are used to produce all colors. The three primary colors of light are:

_____, _____ and _____. ㉕ ㉖ ㉗

Think About:

The Jet Engine

The invention of the jet engine in the 1930's caused a dramatic change in flying. Before jet engines were used, airplanes were driven by propellers. With the power of jet engines, airplanes were suddenly able to fly at amazing new speeds. Jet engines have made it possible for some planes to fly fast enough to break the sound barrier!

Jet engines are built on a principle called jet propulsion. Jet propulsion works much like a balloon that is blown up and then turned loose to fly around as its air escapes. A jet engine sucks in air and mixes it with fuel. The air-fuel mixture burns and creates pressure inside, like a full balloon. The burned gases come out of the engine like the air does as you release a balloon. The engine reacts to this release of pressure by moving forward, as the deflating balloon does.

The forward motion of a jet engine is called **thrust.** The burned gases that come out are called **jet exhaust.**

There are several main kinds of jets: turbojets, pulsejets, ramjets and rockets.

A turbojet is a jet engine which is used in most passenger airplanes. It is much smaller, but more powerful and faster than a propeller engine.

A pulsejet is lighter and simpler than a turbojet. Pulsejets were used in World War II to power missiles.

A ramjet is the simplest of all engines. This engine works best at speeds faster than sound.

A rocket does not use the air around it like other jet engines. It carries its own oxygen needed to burn the fuel. Rockets can work in outer

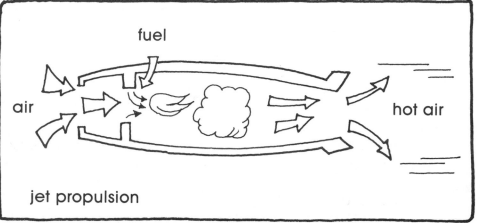

fuel

air

hot air

jet propulsion

space and can fly at very high speeds.

Jet engine airplanes can fly higher and faster than propeller-driven airplanes. Almost all airplanes today are jet powered.

Although real jet engines were first built in the 1930's, the first jet engine was actually designed over 2000 years ago in Egypt. The Chinese used rockets to frighten enemies in 1230. In each century after 1230, people designed or made jet engines. But it wasn't until the mid-1900's that people began to understand how to actually put jet power to use.

• Find the name of the famous person who first broke the sound barrier.

Write.

Jet engines are built on a principle called _____ .

The Jet Engine

Name_____

True or False

_____ The invention of the jet engine caused a dramatic change in flying.

_____ Jet planes were first flown in 1912.

_____ Before jet planes, airplanes were driven by propellers.

_____ Because of jet engines, airplanes could fly much faster.

_____ Propeller planes can fly fast enough to break the sound barrier.

_____ Some jet planes can fly fast enough to break the sound barrier.

Write 1, 2, 3, 4.

How does **jet propulsion** work?

◯ The air-fuel mixture burns and creates pressure.

◯ The engine reacts to this release of pressure by moving forward.

◯ A jet engine sucks in air and mixes it with fuel.

◯ The burned gases come out of the engine.

Match.

thrust   burned gases which are released from a plane

jet exhaust   forward motion of a jet engine

Write, check, circle.

Name four kinds of jets:

_____ _____ _____ _____

A turbojet engine is used in most ☐ propeller ☐ passenger   airplanes.

A turbojet engine is ☐ smaller ☐ larger ☐ faster ☐ more powerful   than a propeller engine.

A pulsejet is lighter and simpler than a _____.

Pulsejets ☐ were used in World War II propeller planes.
         ☐ were used in World War II to power missiles.

A _____ is the simplest of all jet engines.

A ramjet works best at speeds faster / slower than sound.

A rocket does / does not use the air around it, like other jet engines.

A rocket carries its own _____ needed to burn the fuel.

Jet engines were actually designed over _____ years ago in _____.

Think About:

The Space Shuttle

fuel tank

orbiter

USA

rocket boosters

The invention of the Space Shuttle has been a major advancement in space travel. Before the Space Shuttle, rockets which were used to launch spaceships and satellites were not used again. This one-time launching was not only expensive, it also required too much time to prepare a new craft for use.

The Space Shuttle system, which began to operate in the early 1980's, works as a launch vehicle with a big difference. A Space Shuttle can be used again and again. This means that the Space Shuttle greatly reduces the cost of launching flights into space. Without the Space Shuttle system, plans to build spacelabs or space stations would be far too expensive.

A Space Shuttle has three main parts: the orbiter, the fuel tank and rocket boosters.

At liftoff, the rocket boosters blast off with a force that carries the vehicle 27 miles high, at a speed of 3200 miles per hour, in just 126 seconds. At that point, the rockets separate from the orbiter and parachute back to Earth. The rockets are then picked up to be used again.

The orbiter is operated by astronauts as it orbits the Earth and completes its mission. Once the mission is accomplished, the orbiter re-enters the Earth's atmosphere and lands on Earth like a jet airplane.

Space Shuttles are used for different kinds of missions. They may carry scientists into space to conduct experiments. The Space Shuttle can service satellites already in orbit, or retrieve satellites to take back to Earth. The Space Shuttle's cargo bay contains a long robot arm that can move satellites in and out of the orbiter. The cargo bay will hold up to 32,000 pounds on its flight back to Earth.

Upon their return to Earth, Space Shuttles require about two weeks to prepare for a return flight into space.

A Space Shuttle is designed to carry 65,000 pounds of material, such as satellites or spacelabs, in the cargo bay on its trip into space. The materials, called payload, can be anything needed to be used or left in space.

• Tell why you would like to ride on a Space Shuttle.

Write.

The invention of the _____ has been a major advancement in space travel.

Check.

Why was the one-time launching considered to be a problem?

☐ It was too expensive.

☐ It used one craft again and again.

☐ It required too much time to prepare new crafts.

Circle, check, write.

The Space Shuttle

...began to operate in the early   1970's.
                                     1980's.

...is a launch vehicle which can ☐ be disposed of.

                                  ☐ be used again and again.

...greatly reduces the   cost   of launching flights into space.
                         weight

...will make it possible to build _____ in space.

...has three main parts:

the _____, the _____ and the _____.

Write 1, 2, 3, 4.

How does the Space Shuttle work?

○ The rockets separate from the orbiter and parachute back to Earth where they are picked up to be used again.

○ The orbiter is operated by astronauts as it orbits the Earth and completes its mission.

○ At liftoff, the rocket boosters blast off and carry the vehicle miles into space.

○ The orbiter re-enters the Earth's atmosphere and lands on Earth like a jet airplane.

Circle, write, check.

Space Shuttles are used...

to carry   scientists   into space to conduct _____.
           orbits

to service _____ already in orbit.

to retrieve satellites ☐ to take back to Earth.
                        ☐ to use as rockets.

The cargo bay...

☐ contains a long robot arm to move satellites in and out of the orbiter.

☐ contains teams of scientists.

☐ can hold up to 32,000 pounds on its flight back to Earth.

Think About:

The Computer

One of the greatest inventions of the 20th century is the computer. A computer is a device that is used to store and process information and to perform calculations.

A computer can be designed to process almost any type of information. Computers are found in most businesses and industries. They are used in schools, hospitals and libraries. Computers are used by scientists and mathematicians, by doctors and lawyers, and by many other people in many kinds of work.

Computers can do practically anything—except think. Computers can only act on instructions which are entered into their systems; this set of instructions is called a program. A programmer enters instructions into the computer. These instructions are received in a storage unit called the memory. When information is needed, instructions and information are processed by the computer. This information is shown on a screen or printed on paper by a printer or an automatic typewriter.

The computer was not invented by just one person. As early as the 1600's, scientists and mathematicians developed devices for calculations. In the mid-1800's, several machines were developed to calculate numbers by following a set of instructions. But it wasn't until the 1930's and 1940's that electronic computers were designed and built which could compute facts

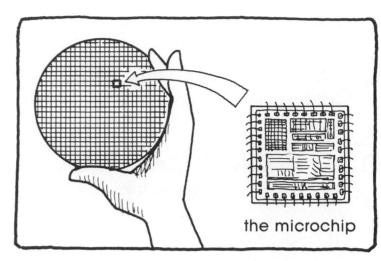

the microchip

in just seconds. The first modern computer was built in 1946; it was known as ENIAC. But this first electronic computer was huge—it required an entire room to hold it.

In 1947, the transistor was invented. With transistors, computers could be made much smaller and more powerful than ENIAC.

But the real breakthrough in computers came in the early 1970's, with the invention of the microchip. A microchip is about the size of a fingernail. The whole microchip unit is called a microprocessor. The microchip holds most of the important parts of a computer.

Because of the microchip, computers can be made much smaller and cheaper. The microchip makes it possible to produce the many microcomputers used today. The programs for microcomputers are called software. The microcomputer itself is called hardware.

Today, microcomputers are used to make everything from video games to space rockets.

● Make a list of things at home, school or in your neighborhood which are operated by microcomputers.

The Computer

Name_____

Write.

A computer is a device that is used to _____ and _____ information

and perform _____.

True and False

Computers...

_____ can be designed to process almost any type of information.

_____ are special machines which are designed to think.

_____ are found in most businesses and industries.

_____ are built to work without further instructions.

_____ are used by scientists, mathematicians, farmers and many others.

_____ can only act on instructions which are placed into their systems.

Write 1, 2, 3, 4.

◯ The instructions are received in a storage unit called memory.

◯ When information is needed, it is processed by the computer.

◯ A programmer enters instructions into the computer.

◯ The information is shown on a screen, or printed on paper.

Underline.

As early as the 1600's...

scientists and mathematicians developed devices for calculation.

scientists designed programs for computers.

In the 1930's and 1940's...

electronic computers were small and easy to use.

electronic computers could compute facts in just seconds.

Circle, write, check.

The first modern computer was built in   1935.

                                                   1946.

The computer was known as _____.

ENIAC was ☐ tiny. ☐ huge. ☐ small enough to sit on a desk.

In 1947, the invention of the _____ made it possible for computers

to be made smaller and more powerful than ENIAC.

In the early 1970's, the invention of the _____ provided the real

breakthrough in computers.

A microchip is about the size of

☐ a desk.   ☐ a book.   ☐ a fingernail.   ☐ a TV.

The whole microchip unit is called a _____.

Think About:

The Laser

The invention of the laser has produced many advances in science. A laser is a special device for strengthening or amplifying light. The light from a laser is not the same as the light from electric bulbs, fluorescent lights or even the sun. Laser light is light that travels in a narrow beam in only one direction.

Because of the strength of laser light, it can be used in many areas, such as, medicine, industry, communications and scientific experiments.

Lasers are important in medicine. Surgeons use the heat of lasers to mend damaged tissue.

Lasers are important in industry. Workers use the intense heat from a laser to melt or cut hard materials. Laser beams are also used to weld metal parts together.

Lasers are important in communications. Laser beams are used to carry television and voice signals over long distances.

Lasers are important in scientific experiments. Lasers are used to make hot gases called plasmas. Plasmas are used to study how energy is made.

There are 3 basic kinds of lasers: solid, gas and liquid.

Solid lasers are used more often than the other kinds of lasers. Solid

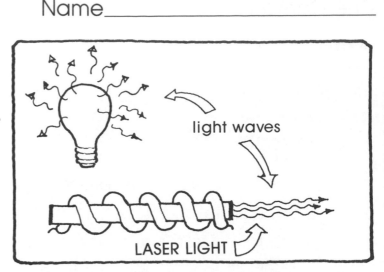

Name _____

light waves

LASER LIGHT

lasers may be made of glass, crystal or a semi-conductor. Solid lasers are used most often in scientific research.

Gas lasers are frequently used in communications. Liquid lasers are used to study atoms and molecules.

The laser was invented in the early 1960's. The invention was possible because of the invention, ten years earlier, of the maser. The maser strengthens or amplifies microwaves. Scientists immediately began working to amplify light waves. In 1960, an American physicist, Theodore H. Maiman, built the first laser.

Lasers are being continually improved. They are even used by astronauts for space experimentation. The astronauts on the Apollo II flight left a laser refractor on the moon. This mirrored device has been used to measure the distance between the Earth and moon.

The word "laser" comes from the term—Light Amplification by Stimulated Emission of Radiation.

- From what you have read, draw a picture of what a laser beam might look like.

Write.

A laser is a special device for _____ and

_____ light.

48   ©1992 Instructional Fair, Inc.

The Laser

Name_____

Write, check.

The light from a laser ☐ is ☐ is not the same as the light from electric
bulbs, fluorescent lights or even the sun.

Laser light travels in a _____ beam in only _____ direction.
Because of the strength of laser light, it can be used in areas, such as:

_____ _____, _____

and _____.

Circle, check, underline, write.

Lasers

In **medicine**, surgeons use the heat
                                    brightness of lasers to:

☐ mend damaged tissue.

☐ warm the surgical instruments.

In **industry,** workers use the heat of lasers to:

☐ melt or cut hard material.

☐ light large storage areas.

☐ weld metal parts together.

In **communications**, laser beams are used . . .

to put more color into televisions.

to carry television and voice signals over long distances.

In **scientific experiments**, lasers are used to make hot gases, called

_____, which are used to study how water is made.
                                              energy

The word **intense** means: ☐ hard, solid material.
                             ☐ to an extremely high or strong degree.

Write.

The three basic kinds of lasers are:

_____, _____ and _____.
       A   B   C

Write A, B, C.

_____ Lasers frequently used in communications

_____ Lasers used most often in scientific research

_____ Lasers used to study atoms and molecules

_____ May be made of glass, crystal or semi-conductor

Write.

The word laser comes from the term: L _____ A _____

by S _____ E _____ of R _____.

Wonder About:

The Pyramids

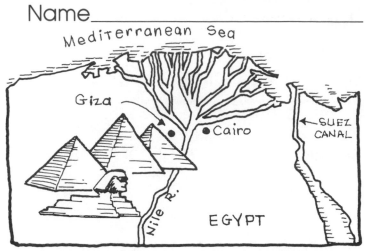

The pyramids of Egypt are among the Seven Wonders of the Ancient World. Pyramids are huge, four-sided, triangular structures which rest on square bases. Pyramids were built in ancient times as tombs or temples for kings or rulers.

The first known Egyptian pyramid was built in 2650 B.C. for King Zoser. It was built by Imhotep, a famous architect, physician and statesman of Egypt. The tomb had an uneven texture and featured a series of giant steps on its sides. This pyramid, called the Step Pyramid, lies near Cairo, Egypt, on the site of the ancient city of Saqqarah.

The largest and most famous of all Egyptian pyramids are located on the west bank of the Nile River near Cairo. Known as the Three Pyramids at Giza, they are the best preserved of all pyramids. The largest of the three pyramids is called the Great Pyramid. It was built in 2600 B.C. as a tomb for King Khufu. The Great Pyramid consists of 2,300,000 blocks of stone, each weighing two and one-half tons. Standing over 450 feet high, its base covers over 13 acres—an area large enough to hold ten football fields.

Since the ancient Egyptians had no iron tools or machinery, they used copper chisels and saws to cut huge blocks of limestone. The blocks were dragged to the pyramids by gangs of workers. Ramps were built on which to drag the blocks of stone up the side of the structure to put in place. An outer layer of white casting stones gave the Great Pyramid a smooth, solid appearance.

Inside the Great Pyramid, corridors lead to several rooms, or chambers. The king's chamber was hewn out of solid stone. It is reached by a 153-foot passage called the Grand Gallery. A second, smaller chamber is called the Queen's Gallery, although the queen was buried in a separate, small pyramid. The third chamber was reached by a 320-foot corridor which descended deep below the ground level of the pyramid.

The other two of the three Pyramids of Egypt lie close by. One was built as a tomb for King Khafre. The other was built for King Mankaure. Near the pyramid of King Khafre stands the famous Sphinx at Giza, built in his honor.

Many of the priceless treasures and mummies buried in the pyramids were later stolen by thieves. Egyptian kings, fearful of this fate, were no longer buried in pyramids. They were buried in secret tombs in cliffs.

• From what you have read, draw a picture showing the chambers and corridors inside the Great Pyramid.

The Pyramids

Name_____

Underline.

The pyramids of Egypt are among the. . .
 Seven Wonders of Ancient Egypt.
 Seven Wonders of the Ancient World.

Check, circle, write.

The pyramids are huge, ☐ five-sided ☐ four-sided, triangular octagonal structures

which rest on _____ bases.

Pyramids were built as tombs palaces or temples for kings.

The **1st** known **pyramid**

. . .was built in _____ B.C. for King _____.

. . .was built by_____, a famous architect in Egypt.

. . .featured a series of giant carvings steps on its sides.

. . .was called the _____.

. . .lies near_____, Egypt, on the site of the ancient city of _____.

the Great Pyramid

. . .was built in _____ B.C. as a tomb for_____.

. . .consists of _____ blocks of stone.

. . .stands over ☐ 450 ☐ 1000 feet high.

. . .has a base which covers over_____ acres.

True or False

Inside the Great Pyramid. . .

_____ corridors lead to several rooms, or chambers.

_____ the King's Chamber was carved from gold.

_____ the King's Chamber is reached by a 153-foot passage.

_____ the queen was buried in the Queen's Gallery.

_____ a 320-foot corridor descends to a third chamber.

Write.

The other two pyramids of the Three Pyramids of Egypt were built as tombs for

King _____ and King _____.

The famous _____ at Giza stands near the pyramid of King Khafre.

Wonder About:

The Hanging Gardens of Babylon

The Hanging Gardens of Babylon are considered to be one of the Seven Wonders of the Ancient World. Built in the late 500's B.C., they were located in the city of Babylon, the capital of the ancient civilization of Babylonia.

The Hanging Gardens were built during the reign of King Nebuchadnezzar II. Historians believe that Nebuchadnezzar had the Hanging Gardens built for his wife Amyitis, who was homesick for her homeland, Media. While Media had been a land of cool, green hills, Babylon was surrounded by dry, flat land. To comfort his wife, Nebuchadnezzar designed a rooftop garden filled with trees and lush gardens.

Ancient historians described the gardens as "vaulted terraces, raised one above the other, resting on cube-shaped pillars." The pillars were hollowed out and filled with earth to allow large trees to be planted. The structure was built with baked brick and stones.

A Babylonian priest of the 200's B.C., named Berossus, described the gardens as rising 75 feet above the ground. The ascent to the top of the gardens was made by stairs. The lush gardens were laid out in terraces covering over 400 square feet.

To grow such trees, shrubs, plants and flowers required almost continuous watering, a difficult task in such hot, arid land. To accomplish this task, water was irrigated from the Euphrates River and lifted to the top of the gardens by a "pumping" system of buckets operated by workers. The watering process never stopped, which provided a constant flow of water through the gardens. The water was drained by layers of reeds and tiles to prevent the water from seeping into the rooms below the garden. Some water was probably allowed to trickle down the walls of the inner rooms to help keep them cool.

In 1899, a German archeologist named Robert Koldeway began excavating a site believed to be the location of ancient Babylonia. Within weeks, he had located what he believed to be the ruins of the Hanging Gardens of Babylon. Underneath this area he discovered a cellar of fourteen rooms, one of which contained a kind of pumping station of wheels and buckets. Koldeway believed this was the remains of the system used to hoist water up to the gardens.

It is hard to imagine how incredible the gardens must have seemed in such dry land.

• Imagine that you live in ancient Babylon. Describe what you would see and think on a visit to the Hanging Gardens.

Hanging Gardens of Babylon

Name_____

Write, check.

The Hanging Gardens were built in the late _____'s B.C.

in the city of ☐ Babylonia. ☐ Babylon.

Babylon was the capital of the ancient civilization _____.

The Hanging Gardens were built during the reign of

King _____ II for his wife, _____.

Amyitis was homesick for her homeland, ☐ Rhodes.
☐ Media.

Match, check.

Media   surrounded by dry, flat land
Babylon   a land of cool, green hills

To comfort his homesick wife, Nebuchadnezzar designed. . .

a ☐ rooftop   garden filled with: ☐ trees   ☐ lush gardens
☐ covered   ☐ statues   ☐ walks

Underline the sentences which tell how an ancient historian described the
gardens.

A Babylonian priest of the 200's B.C., named _____, described the

gardens as . . .

rising _____ feet above the ground.

reached by ascending ☐ ladders ☐ stairs to the top.

laid out on terraces covering over_____ square feet.

To grow the trees, shrubs, plants and flowers, water was irrigated from the

_____ River, and lifted to the gardens by a "_____"
system.

Check, write, circle, underline.

In 1800, a German archeologist located. . .
    1899,

what he believed to be the ruins of the Hanging Gardens.
trees, plants, and shrubs from the Hanging Gardens.

Koldeway found a ☐ palace of ☐ 40 rooms which contained a kind of
☐ cellar   ☐ 14

pumping station of _____ and _____.

Koldeway believed this system was used to ☐ lower ☐ hoist water to the
gardens.

Wonder About:

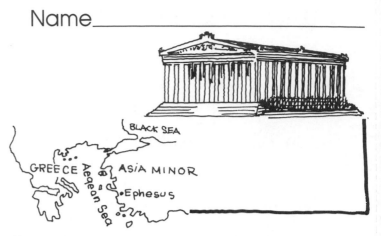

The Temple of Artemis at Ephesus

In the year 1000 B.C., ancient Greeks settled a new colony, called Ephesus, on the coast of Asia Minor across the Aegean Sea from Greece. While the Greeks continued to follow their own customs, over the years they adopted customs of the people of Asia Minor. Through the centuries, they came to worship the goddess Artemis, sometimes called Diana.

A shrine was built in 800 B.C. to honor Artemis. The temple contained a sacred rock which was said to have fallen down from Jupiter. Historians today believe that the rock was a meteorite. The temple was destroyed in 550 B.C. by conquering warriors led by King Croesus of Lydia. King Croesus, known for his great riches, rebuilt the temple and returned it to the people of Ephesus. Over 200 years later, a young Ephesian named Herostratus burned the temple as a way of being remembered in history. To punish Herostratus, it was proclaimed that anyone who spoke his name would be put to death.

The people of Ephesus vowed to rebuild the temple once more in honor of Artemis. The new temple was designed to be more magnificent than ever. Ephesus had become a wealthy and influential city in Asia Minor. Other cities were anxious to send money to Ephesus for the new temple. The greatest builders of the day were hired, the finest materials were used. The greatest sculptor of the time, Scopas of Paros, was in charge of the elaborate plans to rebuild the temple.

Historians disagree, but it is believed to have taken from 80 to 100 years to complete the new temple. The results were so awesome that the temple was declared one of the Seven Wonders of the Ancient World. The temple measured 425 feet long and 225 feet wide. 127 columns, 60 feet high, encircled the temple in double rows. Inside the columns stood the inner temple called the cella. The roof was made of cedar; the doors of cypress. The staircase was carved from a single gigantic vine brought from Cyprus. The centerpiece of the temple was a statue of Artemis.

The Temple of Artemis at Ephesus endured for many centuries. In 133 B.C., the city of Ephesus became part of the Roman Empire. In 262 A.D., the Goths, a barbaric tribe, invaded Ephesus and burned the city to the ground. The only remaining part of the temple was a marble statue of Artemis buried in the ground by Ephesians. It remained buried for centuries until it was discovered by an Austrian archeologist in 1956!

• Find out where the expression, "As rich as Croesus" came from.

The Temple of Artemis at Ephesus

Name_____

Write, circle, check.

In the year 1000 B.C., ancient Greeks settled a new colony, called

_____, on the coast of Asia Minor across the _____ Sea

from Greece.

The Greeks. . .

☐ adopted many customs of the people of Asia Minor.

☐ burned the cities in Asia Minor.

☐ came to worship the goddess Artemis.

The goddess Artemis was also called   ☐ Helena.   ☐ Diana.

1st temple

In 800 B.C., a shrine was built to honor _____.

The temple contained a   statue of Zeus   which was said to have fallen
                          sacred rock

from _____.

Historians today believe the rock was a _____.

The temple was destroyed in   650
                              550   B.C. by warriors led by King _____

of Lydia.

2nd temple

King Croesus. . .   ☐ built a monument to himself.
                    ☐ rebuilt the temple for the people of Ephesus.

Over 200 years later, a young Ephesian named _____

☐ burned the temple as a way of being remembered.

☐ burned the city as a way of being remembered.

To punish Herostratus, it was proclaimed that:

_____.

Underline.

3rd temple – The Temple of Artemis

Ephesus. . .

had become a wealthy and influential city in Asia Minor.

needed money to be able to build a new temple.

The greatest sculptor of the time, _____ of _____, was in charge of

rebuilding the temple.

Wonder About:

The Statue of Zeus at Olympia

One of the most important places in ancient Greece was the holy shrine of Olympia. Olympia was located by Mount Olympus, the home of the chief god, Zeus. For years, no one lived at Olympia except priests and officials who cared for the first small temples. But after the first Olympic Games took place in 776 B.C. on the plains of Olympia, the temples grew in popularity and importance.

The holy shrine of Olympia became the force for bringing many Greeks together for the festival of the Olympic Games every four years. So important were the Olympic Games that the four year cycle of time between the Games was called an Olympiad. Events in Greek life were then spoken of as having occurred in the "fifth Olympiad" or the "twentieth Olympiad."

The holy shrine of Olympia had two main sections: the Stadion, or stadium, where the Olympic Games were held, and the Altis, or sacred grove, where the holy temples were built.

By the fifth century B.C., Olympia was so renowned as a holy place that grand new temples were erected. The most splendid of these was the Temple of Zeus, which contained a statue of Zeus considered to be one of the Seven Wonders of the Ancient World.

The Temple of Zeus was built between 470 and 456 B.C. by Libon, a master architect from nearby Ellis.

The Temple of Zeus towered on a high platform over the grove of the Altis. The temple had thirteen huge columns on each side and six on each end. The white marble of the temple was decorated with red and blue paintings and elaborate carvings. But the showpiece of the temple rested inside. Dominating the inner hall of the temple was the enormous statue of Zeus, the most famous statue in the ancient world. The statue was made by the great Athenian sculptor, Phidias, in 435 B.C. Phidias had also sculpted the great statue of Athena, which stood in the Parthenon on the Acropolis in Athens.

The statue of Zeus was an awesome and majestic sight to all who beheld it. Rising 40 feet tall, it showed Zeus on his throne. The golden throne was set with ivory, ebony and precious stones. Zeus' robe was made of gold and his flesh was carved of ivory. His uplifted right hand held a figurine of Nike, goddess of victory. In his left, he held a scepter made of precious metals.

The temple stood for many years, but was later ordered destroyed by a Roman Emperor.

• How many years would have passed between the 21st and 58th Olympiads?

The Statue of Zeus at Olympia

Name_____

True or False

_____ The holy shrine of Olympia was one of the most important places in ancient Greece.

_____ Olympia was a temple in ancient Athens.

_____ Olympia was located by Mount Olympus.

_____ Mount Olympus was the home of the chief Greek god, Zeus.

_____ For years, only the priests and officials of the temples lived at Olympia.

_____ The first Olympic Games took place in 776 B.C. on the plains of Olympia.

_____ Because of the Olympic Games, no one any longer cared for the temples.

_____ Because of the Olympic Games, the temples grew in popularity and importance.

Check, write.

The Temple of Zeus

. . .was built between _____ and _____ B.C.

. . .was built by_____, a master architect from Ellis.

. . .towered on a high platform

☐ on Mount Olympus. ☐ over the grove of the Altis.

. . .had ____ columns on each side and ____ on each end.

. . .was made of ☐ white ☐ black marble decorated with _____ and

_____ paintings and elaborate carvings.

. . .featured an enormous statue of _____ .

The Statue of Zeus

. . .was the most famous statue ☐ in the ancient world.
☐ of all time.

. . .was made by the great Athenian sculptor,_____, in 435 B.C.

. . .was ☐ 20 ☐ 40 feet tall.

. . .showed Zeus sitting on a golden throne set with _____, _____ and

precious stones.

Underline the sentences which tell what Zeus held in his hands.

The temple was destroyed by a _____ .

Wonder About:

The Lighthouse of Alexandria

By the early 300's B.C., Egypt was no longer ruled by Pharaohs as it was during the age of the pyramids. The country was now ruled by Greeks and Macedonians. The old capital, Memphis, was no longer an important city. Instead, a new capital city, Alexandria, governed most of the country. The new city was named for Alexander the Great, the young Macedonian conqueror who now ruled Egypt.

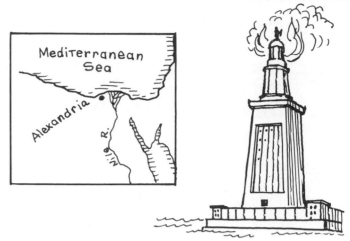

Alexander chose the site for his city in northern Egypt near the Mediterranean Sea. He planned a canal to connect the city with the Nile River, over twenty miles away. This access to two major waterways would allow Alexandria to become an important seaport.

Deinocrates of Rhodes, the most famous architect of the time, was chosen to plan the city. The city he envisioned would have wide streets lined with columns, lush parks and gardens, zoos, museums and libraries. The city was to be a mecca, or attraction, for scholars, merchants, scientists and seamen. It was to become a great trading port and marketplace.

Alexander the Great died in 323 B.C., long before the city could be completed. But one of his successors, Ptolemy, continued the plan for Alexandria. When Ptolemy moved to the completed city, he carried the body of Alexander to be laid to rest in the city which carried his name.

In 290 B.C., Ptolemy ordered the construction of a lighthouse for the city's harbor. The Lighthouse of Alexandria, which stood on the eastern end of the island of Pharos, was designed by the Greek architect, Sostratos. It stood approximately 440 feet high. The Lighthouse was built of three sections. The bottom section, or base, was square. It was used as a military barracks and as a stable for three hundred horses.

The middle section was long and narrow and had eight sides. It featured a balcony where food was sold to travelers who were visiting the lighthouse.

The top section was circular. It contained a beacon chamber where a fire continually burned. The fire's light could be seen over a hundred miles away.

The Lighthouse of Alexandria became so famous that the name of the island, Pharos, became the word used to mean lighthouse.

The lighthouse stood for centuries until about 1375 A.D. when it fell during an earthquake.

- Find out where 3 other cities named Alexandria (also named for Alexander the Great) are located.

The Lighthouse of Alexandria

Name_____

Write, check, circle.

By the early 300's B.C. . . .

Egypt was no longer ruled by _____ .

Egypt was ruled by: ☐ Greeks ☐ Italians
☐ Macedonians ☐ Indians

the old capital, _____ , was no longer an important city.

a new capital, _____ , governed most of the country.

the new capital was named for_____ .

Alexander the Great was a young _____ conqueror who now ruled Egypt.

Alexander chose the site for his city in ☐ southern ☐ northern Egypt, near

the _____ Sea.

He planned a _____ to connect the city with the Nile River over ☐ 200 ☐ 20
miles away.

Alexander believed that this access to two major waterways would allow . . .

☐ a perfect setting for a lighthouse.

☐ the city to become an important seaport.

_____ of Rhodes, the most famous architect of the time, was

chosen ☐ to plan the city.
☐ to build a lighthouse.

He envisioned the city as having:

_____ _____ _____

_____ _____ _____

The city was to be a mecca for:

_____ _____ _____ _____

Alexander died in _____ B.C. before his city could be completed.

One of his successors, _____ , completed the city. Ptolemy ordered the

construction of a _____ for the city's harbor.

The Lighthouse of Alexandria

. . .stood on the ☐ eastern ☐ southern end of the island of _____ .

. . .was designed by the Greek architect _____ .

. . .stood approximately ☐ 440 ☐ 800 feet high.

. . .was destroyed in _____ A.D. by an _____ .

Wonder About:

The Colossus of Rhodes

The Colossus of Rhodes was one of the Seven Wonders of the Ancient World. The word colossus comes from the Greek word colossos, which refers to any statue larger than life size. Although there were many famous larger-than-life statues in the ancient world, only one was given the name Colossus—that was the Colossus of Rhodes.

Rhodes is an island in the Aegean Sea near the southwestern tip of Asia Minor. Its location made it an important place for ships to stop as they sailed back and forth from the Mediterranean and the Aegean Seas. This connection with many parts of the world made Rhodes an extremely developed culture for its time.

In the early 400's B.C., Rhodes was under the control of Athens, Greece. In the 350's B.C., Rhodes was conquered by King Mausolus of Halicarnassus, a city on the coast of nearby Asia Minor. By 332 B.C., Rhodes had been captured by Alexander the Great. After Alexander's death in 323 B.C., his empire was divided into three parts, each governed by one of Alexander's three main generals—Ptolemy, Seleucus and Antigonus.

The island of Rhodes chose to be ruled by Ptolemy, who also ruled Egypt. This angered Antigonus, who decided to punish Rhodes for refusing to choose him as their leader. Antigonus sent his son Demetrius and an army of 40,000 men to capture the island of Rhodes.

For months, Demetrius and his army attacked Rhodes. They used battering rams, catapults and a tower which stood over 150 feet high to try to break into the cities. But the Rhodians held fast, and later, with the help of troops sent by Ptolemy from Egypt, they turned back the attackers.

To show their thankfulness for being saved from their enemies, the people of Rhodes set out to build an enormous statue of Helios, the god of sun.

The great Rhodian sculptor, Chares of Lindos, was given the honor of designing and building the statue. Historians have recorded that the huge bronze statue was begun in 305 B.C. and completed in 292 B.C. It cost almost 18,000 pounds of silver, which would equal approximately five million dollars today. The statue stood almost 120 feet tall—about the same height as the Statue of Liberty.

In 224 B.C., only 68 years after completion, the Colossus of Rhodes was toppled by an earthquake. For centuries, the pieces of the statue lay where they fell. In 653 A.D., conquering Arabs sold the metal pieces of the great statue—for scrap.

• Name another harbor which has a famous statue at its entrance.

The Colossus of Rhodes

Name_____

Write, check.

The word colossus comes from the Greek word _____, which refers to

☐ any Greek statue.

☐ any statue larger than life size.

Rhodes

. . .is an ☐ island ☐ statue   in the _____ Sea, near the

southwestern tip of _____.

. . .was an important place for ships to stop as they sailed back and forth from

the _____ and _____ Seas.

The island of Rhodes chose to be governed by_____, which angered

_____, who:

☐ chose to punish Rhodes for not choosing him.

☐ chose to kill the other two generals.

Antigonus sent his son _____ and an army of

☐ 4,000
☐ 40,000   men to capture the island of Rhodes.

Demetrius and his army attacked Rhodes with _____,

_____ and a _____ which stood over 150 feet high.

Circle, check.

Rhodes, with the help of troops sent from Italy, ☐ turned back the attackers.
Egypt, ☐ was defeated and burned.

To show their thankfulness, the people of Rhodes built an enormous statue of

_____, ☐ the god of war.
☐ the god of sun.

The Colossus of Rhodes

. . .was designed by the great Rhodian sculptor,_____.

. . .was begun in _____ B.C. and completed in _____ B.C.

. . .cost almost _____ pounds of silver, which equals almost

☐ one ☐ five   million dollars.

. . .stood almost _____ feet tall.

. . .was toppled by an ☐ earthquake,
☐ army,   _____ years after it was built.

Wonder About:

The Mausoleum at Halicarnassus

In 337 B.C., a Greek named Mausolus controlled most of southwestern Asia Minor, across the Aegean Sea from Greece. Many of the coastal cities of Asia Minor were inhabited by Greeks. Halicarnassus, the capital city of that region, was 60 miles south of Ephesus, where the great Temple of Artemis was located.

As the king, Mausolus worked hard to develop the city of Halicarnassus, where he lived in a splendid palace with his wife Artemisia. Queen Artemisia was named for the goddess Artemis.

When King Mausolus died in 353 B.C., Queen Artemisia vowed to build the world's most beautiful tomb in his honor.

Messengers carried the word through Greece that the most gifted artists and craftsmen were needed for the project. Scopas, who had guided the construction of the Temple of Artemis at Ephesus, came to Halicarnassus, as did the great architects, Satyros and Pythias. Thousands of other Greeks sailed across the Aegean to Halicarnassus to help build the tomb for Mausolus.

The monument was built high atop a hill overlooking the city. It was surrounded by a huge wall which enclosed a rectangular courtyard. In the center of the courtyard stood a stone platform which could be ascended by a flight of marble steps. The steps were flanked by sculptured lions. The tomb was built on this platform, surrounded by thirty-six columns. A pyramidal structure was built above the tomb. It featured a marble statue of Mausolus in a chariot. The entire building stood over 140 feet high. The completed monument became one of the Seven Wonders of the Ancient World.

Queen Artemisia did not live to see the monument completed. She was buried by her husband in the tomb.

For centuries, the stunning monument stood undisturbed in Halicarnassus. Then, through a series of earthquakes and invasions, most of the structure was toppled. Today, only pieces of the once great building remain.

The tomb for Mausolus was so elaborate and famous that his name has been used to make a new word, mausoleum, which now describes any large tomb. Thus the name, The Mausoleum at Halicarnassus, has been given to one of the Seven Wonders of the Ancient World.

• Which of the other six Wonders of the Ancient World might be called a mausoleum?

62

The Mausoleum of Halicarnassus   Name_____

Write, check, circle.

In 337 B.C., a Greek named _____ controlled most of southwestern

Asia Minor, across the _____ Sea from Greece.

Many of the coastal cities of Asia were inhabited by ☐ Italians. ☐ Greeks.

The capital city of that area was _____.

Halicarnassus was 60 miles south of Athens.
                                     Ephesus.

King Mausolus lived in Halicarnassus with his wife, Queen _____,

who was named for the goddess _____.

Underline, check, write, circle.

When King Mausolus died in ☐ 553 B.C. ☐ 353 B.C.,
    Queen Artemisia vowed to become a great ruler.
    Queen Artemisia vowed to build the world's most beautiful tomb in his honor.

The Mausoleum at Halicarnassus

. . . was built atop a _____ overlooking the city.

. . . was surrounded by a moat
                          huge wall   which enclosed a courtyard.

. . . was reached by ascending a flight of . . .
    ☐ marble steps flanked by sculptures of lions.
    ☐ steps flanked by waterfalls.

. . . featured a marble statue of ☐ Mausolus in a chariot.
                                   ☐ the Greek god, Zeus.

. . . stood over _____ feet high.

Queen Artemisia . . .
    ☐ did not live to see the monument completed.
    ☐ celebrated the completion of the monument with a festival.
    ☐ was buried by her husband in the tomb.

Today, the word **mausoleum** means: ☐ a large tomb.
                                       ☐ a king's monument.

Underline the sentence which tells how the Mausoleum at Halicarnassus was destroyed.

The Mausoleum at Halicarnassus was one of the _____

_____ .

Wonder About:

The Acropolis

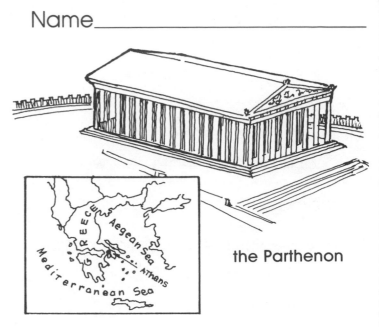

the Parthenon

The Acropolis, located in Athens, Greece, is the site of some of the most famous ruins from an ancient civilization. The word **Acropolis** means "upper city." It refers to the citadel, or highest part of a Greek city, around which the city was built. The hill served as a religious center, and sometimes even a fortress for the city.

The Acropolis in Athens, Greece, rises over 200 feet above the city. During the reign of Pericles, in the 400's B.C., the Parthenon was built on the Acropolis. The Parthenon, today considered the finest building of ancient Greece, was a temple built in honor of Athena, the patron goddess of Athens. The Parthenon, more than 100 feet wide and 230 feet long, is the world's finest example of Doric architecture. The temple was designed by Ictinus and Callicrates. The famous Greek sculptor, Phidias, directed its decoration. The Parthenon, made of white marble, featured a gold and ivory statue of Athena.

The Parthenon stood virtually unchanged for almost a thousand years. In the 500's A.D., it was used as a Christian church. In 1458, it was turned into a mosque by invading Turks. But in 1687, the Parthenon was hit by a shot from a Venetian ship. Gun powder, stored by the Turks in the cellars, exploded and caused great damage.

Today, some of the remaining artwork from the Parthenon is housed in museums. The ruins of the Parthenon still display elaborate carvings of legendary battles between men and centaurs and religious scenes honoring Athena.

Another temple built on the Acropolis, called the Erechtheum, held the oldest known image of Athena.

On the west side of the Acropolis stands the Temple of Athena Nike, which was completed in 424 B.C. Its famous frieze, or carved decorated band, depicts the Battle of Plataea, in which the Greeks defeated the Persians.

Today, these and many other buildings on the Acropolis are being preserved. But many of the statues, ornaments and frescoes no longer remain on the Acropolis. Some have been destroyed over the centuries; others have been taken by invading countries. A few have been removed and are kept in museums.

• Find out more about the goddess Athena and what she meant to the ancient Athenians.

True or False

The Acropolis ...

_____ is located in Athens, Greece.

_____ is a famous seaport in Athens.

_____ means "upper city."

_____ is the highest part of the city.

_____ was used to store the city's food and water.

_____ served as a religious center in ancient Athens.

_____ sometimes served as a fortress for the city.

_____ rises over 1000 feet above the city of Athens.

_____ is the site of famous ruins from ancient Athens.

Check, write, underline.

The most famous building on the Acropolis is called the:

☐ Athena   ☐ Doric   ☐ Parthenon   ☐ Phidias

The Parthenon was built during the reign of _____ in

the   ☐ 500's   ☐ 400's B.C.

The Parthenon is considered to be. . .
   the finest building of ancient Greece.
   the first building of ancient Greece.

The Parthenon was a temple built in honor of _____,

☐ the patron goddess of Athens.   ☐ the goddess of war.

The Parthenon measures over _____ feet wide and _____ feet long.

. . . is the world's finest example of _____ architecture.

. . . was designed by _____ and _____.

. . . was built under the direction of _____,

   ☐ the famous Greek ruler.

   ☐ the famous Greek sculptor.

. . . was made of   ☐ white marble.   ☐ buff limestone.

. . . featured a _____ and _____ statue of ☐ Zeus.
                                                    ☐ Athena.

Underline the sentence which tells what battle is depicted on the frieze in the
   Temple of Athena Nike.

Wonder About:

Stonehenge

On Salisbury Plain, 10 miles north of Wiltshire, England, stands the mysterious prehistoric monument called Stonehenge. The standing group of stones has been the object of speculation and study for centuries. Because of the specific arrangement of the stones, some scholars believe that Stonehenge may have been the site of sun worship or used as an astronomical temple for the study of days, seasons and years.

Archeologists are not sure **why** Stonehenge was built, but they believe they know **how.** The monument appears to be the result of three different construction periods. The first began approximately 1800 B.C. During this time, a circular bank about 327 feet across was built which featured an entrance on the northeast side. Located inside was a circle of 56 pits. They are named the Aubrey Holes for John Aubrey, who discovered them in the 1600's. Outside the entrance stands a 35-ton stone called the Heel Stone.

Almost a century later, the second period of construction began when the first standing stones were added to the monument. These famous blue stones are believed to have come from the Prescelly Mountains over 140 miles away! The stones were placed in two concentric circles (one within the other).

After another century had passed, blocks of sandstone, called sarsen, were brought from the Marlborough Downs over 20 miles away. These 50-ton blocks were used to form a circle of standing stones with horizontal stones lying on top of them. Scientists believe that the builders used stone hammers to produce their work, which included some amazing features. For instance, the top horizontal stones were curved to form the circle. Also, the stones had notches which allowed them to fit exactly on the standing stones. Inside the circle lies a single block, the Altar Stone.

In 1963, Gerald S. Hawkins, from the Smithsonian Observatory, made a study of Stonehenge. He concluded that there was a direct correlation between the placement of the stones and the rising and setting of the sun and moon in the year 1500 B.C. He concluded that Stonehenge may have been built as an astronomical calendar, which could be used to predict seasons of the year, and eclipses of the moon and sun.

Today, the British government is working to restore and protect Stonehenge.

• Imagine that you lived during the time Stonehenge was built. What would you have used Stonehenge for?

66

Stonehenge

Name_____

Write, check.

Stonehenge

. . .is located on _____, 10 miles north of _____,
  England.

. . .is believed to have been the site of ☐ sun worship.
  ☐ many battles.

. . .may have been used as an astronomical temple for the study of

_____, _____ and _____.

Archeologists believe that Stonehenge is the result of ☐ eight ☐ three
  different construction periods.

1st construction period

The first construction period began in ☐ 1800 B.C.
  ☐ 1800 A.D.

A _____ bank, measuring ☐ 300 ☐ 327 feet across, featured an

  entrance on the _____ side.

Located inside was a circle of _____ pits, named the _____.

Outside the entrance stands a _____-ton stone called the _____.

2nd construction period

The second construction period began ☐ 1000 years later.
  ☐ a century later.

The first ☐ carved
  ☐ standing stones were added.

These famous ☐ limestones ☐ bluestones are believed to have come from

  the _____ Mountains over_____ miles away.

The stones are placed in _____ circles.

3rd construction period

The third construction period began. . .

  ☐ after another century had passed.

  ☐ several thousands of years later.

These 50-ton blocks were used to form. . .

  ☐ a building surrounded by 48 columns.

  ☐ a circle of standing stones with horizontal stones lying on top of them.

Inside the circle lies a single block called the _____.

Wonder About:

The Great Wall of China

The Great Wall of China, the longest structure ever built, is one of the most incredible man-made wonders in the world. Constructed entirely by hand, the Great Wall winds 4,000 miles across northern China.

During the 400's B.C., small stretches of the wall were built to protect the country from invaders. During the Ch'in Dynasty, from 221-206 B.C., these first walls were connected together in a new and much longer wall. Work on the wall continued through the Han, Sui and Ming dynasties. It has been estimated that almost a million laborers worked on the Great Wall over a period of many years.

The main part of the Great Wall stretches 2,150 miles long. Special sections of loops and sidewalls add 1,800 more miles to the length of the wall. These sidewalls were added as an extra defense against invaders. The wall is approximately 25 feet high, and 15 feet wide at the top. The core of the wall was made with heavily packed earth. The outer wall was finished with hand-cut stones. For every mile of wall built, over 422,400 cubic feet of material was needed.

To further reinforce the wall, watchtowers were built every 100 to 200 yards in the wall. The towers, which are about 40 feet high, were stocked with food, water and supplies for the defenders on guard at the wall.

Although the Great Wall was built to protect China from invaders, it was only successful with minor attacks. In the 1200's, the army of Genghis Khan, the Mongol leader from the north, swept across the wall and conquered most of China.

Over the centuries, much of the Great Wall deteriorated. Today, three main sections of the wall have been rebuilt. One section is near the city of Peking. Another is in the province of Kansu in north-central China. The third restored section is along the country's east coast.

The Great Wall no longer exists for defense. Instead, it has become a tourist attraction for people from all around the world.

• Write a paragraph telling why you think the Great Wall was not successful in protecting China against invaders.

Write, circle.

The Great Wall winds _____ miles across southern / northern China.

Name_____

Write, check.

Work on the wall continued through the _____, _____ and _____ Dynasties.
Almost a ☐ million ☐ half-million   laborers worked on the Great Wall.

The Great Wall

. . .consists of a main section which is _____ miles long.

. . .has special loops and sidewalls which add _____ more miles to its length.

. . .had sidewalls as extra ☐ defense ☐ artillery   against invaders.

. . .is approximately _____ feet high and _____ feet wide at the top.

. . .has a core of ☐ heavily packed earth. ☐ packed sand.

. . .has an outer wall made of hand-cut _____ .

Underline.

For every mile of wall built. . .
    over 422,400 cubic feet of material was needed.
    over 200,000 laborers were needed.

Circle, check, write.

To further reinforce the wall   watch towers / military bases   were built every _____ to _____ yards.

Standing about ☐ 100 ☐ 40   feet high, the towers were stocked with

_____ , _____ and _____ .

Underline.

Why was the Great Wall of China built?
    To display China's borders to the rest of the world
    To protect China from invaders

Write, circle.

In the 1200's, the army of _____, the   Mongol / Greek   leader from the north,
    swept over the wall and conquered China.

Today,   eight / three   main sections of the wall have been rebuilt.

Where are these sections located?

    1. _____

    2. _____

    3. _____

Underline the sentence which tells what the Great Wall is used for today.

Wonder About:

Angkor Wat

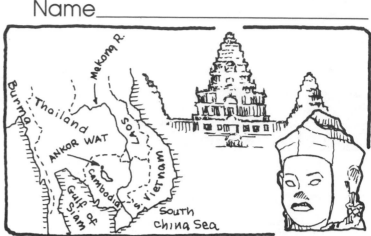

One of the most incredible man-made wonders in the world is located deep in the jungles of Cambodia in Southeast Asia. The religious complex called Angkor Wat covers one square mile of land and contains temples and towers laid out in a pyramidal style.

Angkor Wat was built in the 1100's by the Cambodian King, Suryavarman II. He ordered the temple built in honor of the Hindu god, Vishnu. Suryavarman II was later buried in Angkor Wat.

Angkor Wat is considered to be the finest architectural monument in Cambodia. Its style was designed to resemble the mythological home of the Hindu gods. One temple alone displays over 1,500 columns, carved from a mountain over 30 miles away.

Angkor Wat can be entered by crossing a bridge that lies over a moat. The bridge leads to a three-tiered stone wall that stretches two-and-one-half miles long and 600 feet wide. Past this wall lies a short road that leads into the main grounds of the temple. The road is lined with ornately carved sculptures of seven-headed snakes.

The main temple is crowned with five huge towers which represent the five peaks of Mount Meru. Mount Meru is described in Hindu mythology as standing 80,000 leagues high in the center of the earth.

Angkor Wat, built with buff and pink limestone, was created in such a way to look as if it were a large mountain of rock which had been carved with designs, instead of a building made of stones.

Many of the carvings on the temples of Angkor Wat depict scenes from early Cambodian history. Other carvings show mythical creatures, gods and goddesses.

Through the centuries, the humid air has caused damage to parts of Angkor Wat. But since the early 1900's, Cambodian and French archeologists have worked together to restore the buildings.

● From reading the story, draw a picture showing what the road leading to the temple might look like.

Underline.

Angkor Wat . . .

    is considered to be the oldest structure in Cambodia.

    is considered to be the finest architectural monument in Cambodia.

Angkor Wat

Name_____

Write, check, circle.

What was Angkor Wat built to resemble? _____

_____

One temple of Angkor Wat displays over ☐ 1500 ☐ 2500 columns carved from a mountain ☐ in central China. ☐ over 30 miles away.

Angkor Wat is entered by a bridge / tunnel which lies over a jungle. / moat.

The stone wall surrounding Angkor Wat is:

☐ three-tiered   ☐ embedded with jewels   ☐ 600 feet wide

☐ two-and-one-half miles long   ☐ guarded by soldiers

Underline.

The road leading to the main temple is lined with . . .
    ornate sculptures of seven snakes.
    ornate sculptures of seven-headed snakes.

Write.

What do the five huge towers of the main temple represent? _____

_____

Underline the sentence which tells how Mount Meru was described in Hindu mythology.

True or False.

_____ Angkor Wat was built with buff and pink limestone.

_____ Angkor Wat was built to look like a group of modern buildings.

_____ Carvings on the temples show scenes from Cambodian history and mythological creatures.

_____ Angkor Wat has been allowed to deteriorate without repairs.

Check.

The word **restore** means:

☐ to bring back to an original condition.

☐ to deteriorate and fall apart.

Modern Wonder: Eiffel Tower

The Eiffel Tower in Paris, France, is considered to be one of the Seven Wonders of the Modern World. The Eiffel Tower stands 984 feet high. It is made of a wrought-iron framework which rests on a base that is 330 feet square. The tower is made of 12,000 pieces of metal and 2½ million rivets. Elevators and stairways lead to the top of the tower. Among other things, the Eiffel Tower contains restaurants and weather stations. Since 1953, it has been used as the main television transmitter for Paris. Before that, it was used to transmit radio signals, and as a weather monitoring station.

Today, everyone agrees that the Eiffel Tower is a true wonder. But in 1887, many people believed that Alexander Gustave Eiffel was crazy when he began building his metal tower.

Gustave Eiffel designed his tower to be the centerpiece of the World's Fair Exposition of 1889 in Paris. He was chosen for the project because he was, at age fifty-three, France's master builder. Eiffel was already famous for his work with iron, which included the framework for the Statue of Liberty.

On January 26, 1887, workers began digging the foundation for the Eiffel Tower. Practically everyone but Gustave Eiffel believed that it would be impossible to finish what would be the tallest structure in the world in just two years. After all, it had taken 36 years to build the Washington Monument. Furthermore, the French government would only grant the project one-fifth of the money needed. Eiffel himself agreed to provide 1.3 million dollars which he could recover if the tower was a financial success.

In March of 1889, after over two years of continuous work, the Eiffel Tower was completed. Eiffel had not only met his deadline, but he had built the tower for less money than he had thought it would cost. The final cost was exactly $1,505,675.90.

When Gustave Eiffel died in 1923, the Eiffel Tower was still the tallest manmade structure in the world. Today, several buildings have surpassed the Eiffel Tower in height. But the Eiffel Tower, standing on the Champ de Mars in Paris, is still the tallest **tower** in the world!

• Write a story describing people watching the Eiffel Tower being built.

Write.

. . . is located in _____, France.

Write.

The **Eiffel Tower** . . .

stands _____ feet high.

is made of a _____—_____ framework.

rests on a base that is _____ feet square.

is made of _____ pieces of metal.

contains _____ rivets.

contains _____ and _____ that lead to the top.

Check, circle.

What has the Eiffel Tower been used for?

☐ television transmitter ☐ weather monitor

☐ oil-drilling rig ☐ radio transmitter

The Eiffel Tower contains   restaurants   and   weather balloons.
                            bookstores   weather stations.

True or False

_____ The Eiffel Tower was designed for the World's Fair Exposition of 1899.

_____ Many people thought the Eiffel Tower could not be built.

_____ Gustave Eiffel was a well-known artist in Paris.

_____ Workers began digging the foundation on January 26, 1887.

_____ The Eiffel Tower took 3 years and 2 months to complete.

_____ At age fifty-three, Gustave Eiffel was France's masterbuilder.

_____ Gustave Eiffel had also designed the Washington Monument.

Check.

How much money did the French Government grant?

☐ 100 percent of the money needed

☐ 1.3 million dollars

☐ one-fifth of the money needed

Underline the sentence in the story which tells how much money Gustave Eiffel agreed to provide.

Write.

The final cost of the Eiffel Tower was $__,__ __ __,__ __ __.__ __ .

Write.

When Gustave Eiffel died in 1923, the Eiffel Tower was still . . .

_____ .

Today, the Eiffel Tower is still . . .

_____ .

Wonder About:

Taj Mahal

The Taj Mahal is one of the most beautiful and elaborate man-made wonders in the world. It is located in the city of Agra in northern India.

Almost four centuries ago, in 1612, the Indian ruler Shah Jahan married an Indian princess. Shah Jahan called his wife Mumtaz-i-Mahal, which means, "pride of the palace." In 1631, Mumtaz-i-Mahal died. Her grieving husband decided to build an extravagant mausoleum, or tomb, for his wife and himself. He chose the banks of the Jumma River as the location for his monument.

It took more than 20,000 workers to build the Taj Mahal between the years of 1632 and 1653. The plans were drawn by a committee of architects from India, Persia and many parts of Asia.

The Taj Mahal is surrounded by walls which enclose rows of formal gardens and reflecting pools lined with cypress trees. These gardens lead to the mausoleum, which stands in the center of the grounds with two smaller buildings on either side.

The Taj Mahal, made of white marble, stands on an eight-sided platform made of red sandstone. Each side of the platform is 130 feet long. Each corner of the platform features a three-story, 138-foot-tall praying tower, called a minaret.

The mausoleum itself is almost 200 feet square. A great arch over 108 feet high is cut into each side of the building. The center part of the building is covered by a huge dome. The exterior of the building is decorated with passages from the Koran, the Moslem holy book.

Inside the Taj Mahal, elaborate decorations fill the walls. Precious stones, such as jasper, bloodstone, agates, cornelians and jade are inlaid in the marble walls to form pictures. In some cases, over 100 stones are used just to make one flower.

Marble walls of trelliswork, or carved designs, allow the sunlight to filter through the building in a soft glow. A center room contains two monuments called cenotaphs. A vault below the monuments holds the bodies of Shah Jahan and his wife.

• Find the names of three other famous tombs.

Write, check, circle.

The Taj Mahal is located in the city of _____, in northern ☐ France. ☐ India.

Almost four centuries ago, in 1612, the Indian ruler,_____, married
an Indian princess. 1812,

Taj Mahal

Name_____

Shah Johan called his wife _____, which means

"_____ of the _____."

In 1631, Mumtaz-i-Mahal ☐ died. ☐ married.

The Taj Mahal was built as a ☐ mausoleum ☐ palace   for Mumtaz-i-Mahal.

Shah Jahan chose the banks of the _____ River as the location for the
Taj Mahal.

It took more than _____ workers to build the Taj Mahal between the

years of _____ and _____.

The word **mausoleum** means: ☐ palace. ☐ tomb.

Underline.

The plans for the Taj Mahal were drawn by . . .
        a committee of architects from India, Persia and Asia.
        a committee of Indian rulers.

Write, check.

The Taj Mahal

. . . is made of ☐ carved jade. ☐ white marble.

. . . stands on an eight-sided platform made of _____ _____.

. . . features 138-foot-tall praying towers, called _____.

. . . is almost ☐ 500 ☐ 200 feet square and is covered by a huge _____.

. . . is decorated with passages from the ☐ Koran. ☐ legends of India.

Check, write, circle.

The **Koran** is ☐ the ruler of India. ☐ the Moslem holy book.

The inside of the Taj Mahal is decorated with pictures made of precious stones,

such as _____.

_____

In some pictures, over _____ stones are used to make one flower.

A center room contains two monuments called   vaults.
                                               cenotaphs.

Underline the sentence which tells who is buried in the Taj Mahal.

Wonder About:

Suez Canal

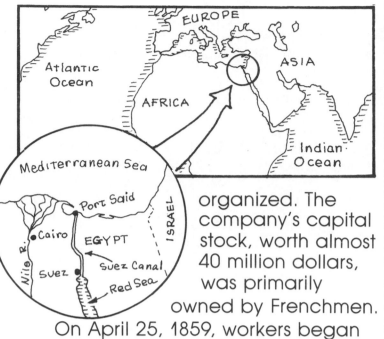

The development of the Suez Canal, a narrow, artificial waterway, was a modern man-made wonder of great significance. The waterway covers over 100 miles in Egypt to connect the Mediterranean Sea and the Red Sea. Because of the canal, which opened in 1869, the route between England and India was shortened by over 6,000 miles. The Suez Canal extends north and south through the Isthmus of Suez. It opens into the Mediterranean Sea at the city of Port Said and into the Red Sea at the city of Suez. Unlike many canals, the Suez Canal does not require locks, since the levels of the two seas are not significantly different.

When the Suez Canal was first built, it measured 230 feet wide and 26 feet deep. Since then, it has been enlarged to handle larger ships. Today, it measures 390 feet wide and 46 feet deep.

In 1799, Napolean I first suggested a canal across the Isthmus of Suez after he visited Egypt. A French builder, Ferdinand de Lesseps, was put in charge of the plans. He received permission from Muhammad Said, the Viceroy of Egypt, to proceed with the project. The next year, an International Technical Commission met to decide on the exact route of the canal. A company to finance the project was organized. The company's capital stock, worth almost 40 million dollars, was primarily owned by Frenchmen.

On April 25, 1859, workers began construction of the Suez Canal. Ten years later, on November 17, 1869, the canal was officially opened.

Although Great Britain was a primary user of the Suez Canal, it did not buy shares of stock in the company until 1875. It then began sharing management responsibilities with France.

Although an international commission ruled that the canal would be open to all nations, during World Wars I and II, the canal was closed to enemies of Great Britain.

Until November 6, 1956, the United States, Great Britain, France, Israel and Egypt were not in agreement on how to control the canal. At that time, the United Nations stepped in and settled the dispute. In March of 1957, the canal was placed under the management of Egypt.

● Write a paragraph telling how different water travel would be without the Suez Canal.

The Suez Canal

Check, write, circle.

The Suez Canal

. . . is a narrow, artificial ☐ waterway. ☐ harbor.

. . . covers over _____ miles in _____ to connect these two seas:

☐ Mediterranean ☐ Baltic ☐ Nile ☐ Red ☐ Arctic

. . . shortened the route between England / Sweden and China / India by _____ miles.

. . . extends west / north and south / east through the Isthmus of _____.

. . . opens into the Mediterranean Sea at the city of _____.

. . . opens into the Red Sea at the city of _____.

Underline the sentence which tells why the canal does not require locks.

Write 1-8.

How did the **Suez Canal** begin?

◯ Muhammad Said gave permission for the project to proceed.

◯ A company to finance the canal project was organized.

◯ In 1799, Napolean I proposed a canal after he visited Egypt.

◯ On November 17, 1869, the canal was officially opened.

◯ Company stock, worth 40 million dollars, was primarily owned by Frenchmen.

◯ A French builder, Ferdinand de Lesseps, was put in charge of the plans.

◯ An International Technical Commission met to decide on the canal's route.

◯ On April 25, 1859, workers began construction on the canal.

True or False

_____ In 1875, Great Britain began sharing management responsibilities with France.

_____ The canal was intended to be open to only five nations.

_____ During World Wars I and II, the canal was closed to enemies of Great Britain.

_____ On November 6, 1956, the United Nations settled a dispute between Israel and Italy.

_____ In March of 1957, the canal was placed under the management of Egypt.

Wonder About:

Panama Canal

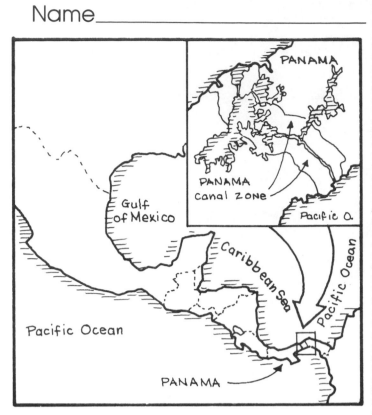

When the Panama Canal was completed in 1914, it became one of the greatest engineering wonders in the world. Built by the United States, the canal is a waterway which cuts across the Isthmus of Panama to link the Atlantic Ocean and the Pacific Ocean.

Prior to the opening of the Panama Canal, ships traveling from one ocean to the other were forced to sail around South America. The canal meant that a ship sailing between New York and San Francisco would sail approximately 5000 miles, instead of the 13,000 miles required before the canal was opened.

For hundreds of years, people had known of the importance of a waterway across Central America. In 1903, the United States signed a treaty with Panama, which allowed the United States to build and operate a canal.

One of the first obstacles to overcome in building the canal was disease, which plagued the Isthmus of Panama. Special medical teams were sent to the area to improve sanitary conditions. Efforts were made to rid the area of mosquitoes which carried malaria and yellow fever.

In 1906, it was decided that the canal would be built by a series of locks, which would be cheaper and quicker to build. In 1907, an army engineer, Colonel George Goethals, was put in charge of the project. Construction began with three main tasks: to excavate tons of earth to clear passages, to build a dam across the Chagres River and create a new lake, and to build the series of locks.

Thousands of workers used steam shovels and dredges to cut passages through hills, swamps and jungles.

The completed canal was built at a cost of 380 million dollars. It runs 50 miles across the Isthmus of Panama from Limon Bay in the Atlantic to the Bay of Panama in the Pacific. The water in the canal is controlled by three sets of locks, or water-filled chambers. Each lock is 1,000 feet long, over 100 feet wide and 70 feet deep. All but the very largest of today's ships can pass through the canal.

In 1977, a new treaty was signed which made most of the canal zone part of Panama.

• Draw a map showing the route a ship would take from the Atlantic to the Pacific if there were no Panama Canal.

Panama Canal

. . .was completed in ☐1904. ☐1914.

. . .became one of the greatest engineering   wonders in the world.
                                 natural

. . .was built by the ☐ country of Panama.
                       ☐ United States.

. . .cuts across the _____ of _____.

. . .links the _____ Ocean and the _____ Ocean.

Circle, write, check.

In 1803, the United States signed a treaty with _____,
    1903,

   which allowed Panama to build and operate a canal.

   which allowed the United States to build and operate a canal.

One of the first obstacles to overcome in building the canal was_____,
   which plagued the Isthmus of Panama.

Special medical teams were sent:

   ☐ to improve sanitary conditions.

   ☐ to build ten new hospitals.

Efforts were made to rid the area of ☐ wasps,   which carried
                                      ☐ mosquitoes,

_____ and _____.

In 1906, it was decided that the canal would be built by a series of _____.

In 1907, Colonel _____ was put in charge of the project.

Construction began with three major tasks:

   1. _____

   2. _____

   3. _____

The word **excavate** means: ☐ to form a waterway.
                              ☐ to dig or scoop out earth.

The completed canal. . .

   was built at a cost of _____ million dollars.

   runs ☐ 500   miles across the Isthmus of Panama, from _____
         ☐ 50

      in the Atlantic to the _____ of _____ in the Pacific.

Wonder About:

The Brooklyn Bridge

When the Brooklyn Bridge was opened on May 24, 1883, it was declared to be the "Eighth Wonder of the World." Spanning the East River in New York City, the Brooklyn Bridge joined the boroughs, or districts, of Brooklyn and Manhattan. At its opening, it was the longest suspension bridge on Earth. The bridge, with a span of 1595 feet, cost a total of 15 million dollars to build. The Brooklyn Bridge hangs, or is suspended, from huge steel cables approximately 16 inches thick. The cables are fastened to two gothic-style towers which stand 275 feet high at each end of the bridge. The bridge holds six lanes of traffic in addition to a unique walkway down its middle.

The building of the Brooklyn Bridge was one of the greatest architectural achievements ever. The credit belonged to a father and son, John A. Roebling and Colonel Washington A. Roebling. The Roeblings were pioneer builders of big suspension bridges. Prior to the Brooklyn Bridge, wrought iron had been used to support bridges. The Roebling's plan called for their new bridge to be built with steel-wire cables.

To hold the cables, the Roeblings had to first construct two large towers. These towers were built on huge foundations which were sunk in the riverbed and filled with concrete.

By 1877, the towers were completed, and work had begun on "spinning the cables." This process involved bunching steel wires together in compact bundles to form four, 16-inch cables. These cables were used to hold more than 1500 smaller cables which reached down to hold the bridge.

By the time the bridge opened in 1883, after 14 years of construction, twenty workers had died in accidents while building the bridge. John A. Roebling had also died as the result of an injury he had received while surveying the tower site. His son, Washington, managed to continue overseeing the project, but not without his own health problems. He developed the bends from working deep inside the bridge towers' bases. For months, he was confined to bed where he viewed the bridge (a quarter mile away) through his telescope. With the help of his wife, he still managed to supervise the completion of the bridge.

Today, the Brooklyn Bridge is still considered to be among the greatest engineering feats of all time.

• Find the names of three other famous suspension bridges.

The Brooklyn Bridge

Name_____

Write, check.

When the Brooklyn Bridge was opened on May 24, _____, it was declared to

be the "_____ of the _____."

The Brooklyn Bridge spans the ☐ East ☐ Hudson River in _____City.

The bridge joins the boroughs, or districts, of _____ and _____.

Underline.

At its opening, the Brooklyn Bridge...
    was the only suspension bridge on Earth.
    was the largest suspension bridge on Earth.

Write, check.

The bridge was built by a father, _____, and his son,

Colonel _____ .

The Roeblings...
    ☐ were pioneer builders of big suspension bridges.
    ☐ were also the builders of the Statue of Liberty.

Prior to the Brooklyn Bridge, _____ had been used to
support bridges.

The Roeblings plan called for the new bridge to be built with _____ cables.

The cables were held by ☐ steel beams.
                   ☐ two large towers.

Underline, write.

The cables were made by...
    bunching steel wires together in compact bundles.
    cutting sections of steel rods.

The cables were used to hold more than _____ smaller cables which reach
down to hold the bridge.

Match.

John A. Roebling...   supervised the completion of the bridge.
Washington A. Roebling...   died before the bridge was completed.

Underline the sentence which tells how many workers died during the 14-year
construction period.

Wonder About:

Yellowstone National Park

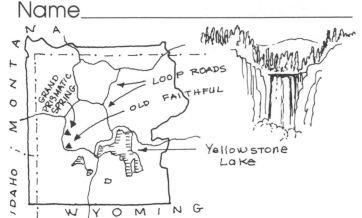

The Yellowstone National Park, located in the western United States, is the site of some of the most famous natural wonders in the world: geysers, hot springs, deep canyons, waterfalls and great evergreen forests. Yellowstone, the oldest national park in the United States, covers an area of land some 60 by 50 miles. Most of the land is located in the state of Wyoming, but it also spreads into Idaho and Montana. Scientists believe that the landscape of Yellowstone was created by a series of volcanic eruptions thousands of years ago. Molten rock, called magma, remains under the park. The neat from the magma produces the 200 geysers and thousands of hot springs for which Yellowstone is most famous.

Of all the wonders in Yellowstone, the main attraction is the famous geyser, Old Faithful. Approximately every 65 minutes, Old Faithful erupts for a period of three to five minutes. The geyser erupts in a burst of boiling water that jumps 100 feet in the air. Other geysers in the park produce a spectacular sight, but none are as popular as Old Faithful.

Geysers may differ in frequency of eruption and size, but they all work in much the same way. As water seeps into the ground, it collects around the hot magma. The heated water produces steam which rises and pushes up the cooler water above it. When the pressure becomes too great, the water erupts into the air. The cooled water falls back to the ground and the cycle begins again.

The magma under the park also produces bubbling hot springs and bubbling mud pools, called mudpots. The largest hot spring in Yellowstone, Grand Prismatic Spring, measures 370 feet.

Yellowstone Lake, which measures over 20 miles long and 14 miles wide, is the largest high altitude lake in North America. It lies almost 8,000 feet above sea level.

Ninety percent of Yellowstone Park is covered by evergreen forests of pine, fir and spruce trees. 200 species of birds are found in Yellowstone. More than 40 kinds of other animals live in Yellowstone, which is the largest wildlife preserve in the United States. Visitors to the park can see bears, bison, cougars, moose and mule deer.

The Yellowstone National Park offers more than 1,000 miles of hiking trails. More than two million persons visit the park each year.

• Write about safety tips for camping out in Yellowstone National Park.

82

Yellowstone National Park

Name_____

Circle, check, write.

The Yellowstone National Park is the ⟨oldest / warmest⟩ park in the United States.

Yellowstone National Park covers an area of
☐ 5 square miles.
☐ 60 by 50 miles.

Most of Yellowstone National Park is located in the state of:
☐ California   ☐ Idaho   ☐ Wyoming   ☐ Utah

The park also spreads into the states of _____ and _____.

Name some of the famous natural wonders found at Yellowstone. _____

_____

_____

Scientists believe that the landscape of Yellowstone was created:

☐ by water erosion for thousands of years.

☐ by a series of volcanic eruptions thousands of years ago.

Molten rock, called _____, lies under the park's soil.

The most popular attraction at Yellowstone is _____.

This attraction is a ☐ waterfall ☐ geyser   which erupts every _____ minutes

for a period of _____ to _____ minutes.

Old Faithful's eruption sends boiling water

☐ across the park in winding streams.

☐ 100 feet in the air.

Write 1-5.

How is a geyser formed?

◯ The water, heated by the magma, produces steam.

◯ When the pressure becomes too great, the water erupts into the air.

◯ Water seeps into the ground and collects around the hot magma.

◯ The cooled water falls back to the ground.

◯ The steam rises and pushes the cooler water above it.

Check, write.

The magma also produces:
☐ hot springs ☐ canyons
☐ mud pools ☐ gardens

The largest hot spring in Yellowstone is _____ _____,

which measures ☐ 200 ☐ 370 feet.

Wonder About:

Carlsbad Caverns

Carlsbad Caverns are among the most phenomenal natural wonders in the world. The underground system of caves and tunnels is believed to be the largest underground labyrinth in the world. Located about 20 miles southwest of Carlsbad, New Mexico, the Carlsbad Caverns extend for **at least** 23 miles.

Scientists believe that the caverns were formed as water penetrated and dissolved the underground limestone. The caverns extend at least 1,100 feet below ground. They display thousands of beautiful stalactites, hanging from the ceiling, and stalagmites, rising from the floor. These formations are made of aragonite and calcite, crystalline limestone which have built up over the years. The caverns receive their shades of red, yellow and tan from small amounts of iron ore and other minerals.

The largest area in the caverns is called the Big Room. It measures 1,300 feet long, 650 feet wide, and 300 feet high. The Big Room features rock formation called Rock of Ages and a 60-foot tall stalagmite called the Giant Dome. Other chambers are named King's Palace, Queen's Chamber, Green Lake Room and Papoose's Chamber.

For centuries, the entrance to the caverns, Bat Cave, was known to the Indians of that area. In 1901, a miner named James L. White discovered the caves. Because of his further explorations and enthusiasm, the caverns became known to the rest of the country. On October 25, 1923, the Carlsbad Caverns were made a national monument. Later, the National Geographic Society organized a series of scientific explorations of the caverns. On May 14, 1930, the area was declared to be Carlsbad Caverns National Park. Originally, the park covered 700 acres. Today, it covers 73 square miles.

Visitors to Carlsbad Caverns are given a guided tour which begins at the natural entrance and covers a three mile route. Visitors can ride an elevator from the entrance directly to the underground lunchroom, located near the Big Room.

One of the most incredible sights for visitors to see occurs outside the caverns. Each night during the summer months, millions of bats fly out of the Bat Cave entrance. During the daytime, they hang in the cave on the walls and ceilings. But at night, they leave the cave to find food. It is believed that each night the bats consume 11½ tons of insects!

- Imagine that you have discovered a cave. List five safety tips for exploring this new-found cave.

84

Carlsbad Caverns

Name_____

Write and underline.

Carlsbad Caverns are a system of _____ and _____ . . .

    which form the largest underground labyrinth in the world.

    which were formed within the last five hundred years.

Check.

The word **labyrinth** means:

☐ a system of passages much like a maze.

☐ an enormous, undergound cave.

Write, check.

Carlsbad Caverns

. . .are located _____ miles southwest of Carlsbad, New Mexico.

. . .extend underground for at least _____ miles.

. . .are believed to have formed . . .

☐ as the air decayed the rock and caused it to fall away.

☐ as water penetrated and dissolved the underground limestone.

. . .receive their colors of _____ , _____ and _____ from small

    amounts of ☐ iron ore ☐ gold and other minerals.

The caverns display beautiful formations called _____ , which

    hang from the ceiling, and _____ , which rise from the floor.

These formations are made of crystalline limestone named _____

    and _____ .

The largest area in the caverns is called the ☐ Bat Cave.
  ☐ Big Room.

The area measures: _____ feet long

            _____ feet wide

            _____ feet high

Check, write.

On October 25, 1923, Carlsbad Caverns became a:

☐ scientific reserve. ☐ national monument.

On May 14, 1930, the area was named _____

_____ .

Underline the paragraph which tells of the incredible sight seen each summer
night at the entrance to the caverns.

Wonder About:

Mount Rushmore National Memorial

One of the most famous and recognizable manmade wonders of the world Is found on Mount Rushmore in the Black Hills of South Dakota. Mount Rushmore National Memorial is a huge carving on a granite cliff which shows the faces of four of America's greatest presidents: George Washington, Thomas Jefferson, Theodore Roosevelt and Abraham Lincoln.

Mount Rushmore is located 25 miles from Rapid City, South Dakota. The cliff rises over 500 feet above the valley, and is 5,725 feet above sea level.

On August 10, 1927, thousands of people gathered at the base of Mount Rushmore to witness the first drilling on the mountainside by the man chosen to design and supervise the memorial, Gutzon Borglum. Borglum was a well-known sculptor, famous for his excellent technique and creativity. His previous works included the statue of Lincoln's head, located in the Capitol in Washington, D.C., and another statue of Lincoln seated on a bench, located in Newark, New Jersey. His statue, Mares of Diomedes, is displayed in the Metropolitan Museum of Art in New York.

Borglum began work on the monument by dividing the carving into a series of steps. The first step, called pointing, was an exact drawing of each president's head which showed the precise place for putting each drill in the rock and the exact depth to which each drill could go.

The workers used "swing seats," invented by Borglum, to hang over the side of the cliff. From these seats, they were able to drill at each exact point. After drilling, the holes were filled with a certain amount of dynamite, which was detonated each day when all of the workers were off the mountain. By the completion of the memorial, over 450,000 tons of granite had been blasted away.

The first president to be finished was George Washington. His carved head was over 60 feet tall—as high as a five-story building. The work continued another eleven years until all four presidents were completed.

Borglum did not live to see the entire monument completed. After his death in 1941, his son, Lincoln, finished the famous project which his father had begun.

The unique memorial took 14 years and one million dollars to complete. Today, it stands as a national symbol which scientists predict can last for some five million years to come.

• If you were designing a new Mount Rushmore, which four presidents would **you** choose, and why?

86

Mount Rushmore National Memorial   Name_____

Write, check.

Mount Rushmore National Memorial is located in the _____ Hills of

_____.

It is a huge carving on a ☐ granite ☐ grassy cliff which shows the faces of

_____ American presidents. The presidents are:

_____

Write, check.

The man chosen to design and supervise the memorial was _____,

☐ a well-known sculptor.

☐ a well-known mountaineer.

Some of Borglum's previous works were:

1. _____

2. _____

3. _____

Yes or No

Pointing . . .

_____ was an exact drawing of each president's head.

_____ was a seat designed to hang over the cliff.

_____ showed the precise place for putting each drill in the rock.

_____ showed the exact depth each drill should go.

The workers used "_____ seats" ☐ to store the dynamite.
☐ to hang over the side of the cliff.

Write 1, 2, 3, 4.

◯ Sitting in swing seats, the workers drilled at each exact point.

◯ When the workers were off the mountain, the dynamite was detonated.

◯ The workers used pointing to mark the exact site for drilling.

◯ The holes were filled with a certain amount of dynamite.

Check, write, circle.

The word **detonate** means: ☐ to cause to explode.
☐ to drill.

By the completion of the memorial, over _____ tons of granite had
been blasted away.

Borglum did / did not live to see the memorial completed.

His son, _____, finished the project.

Wonder About:

The Sequoia

One natural wonder of the world is among the oldest and largest of living things on Earth. It is the sequoia, a tree that once grew in plentiful varieties in forests over much of the world. Today, sequoias are found mainly in California, where only two kinds of true sequoias—the redwood and the giant sequoia—still grow.

The redwood, which is the tallest living tree, is found in the coastal mountains of northern California and southern Oregon. Growing in this warm, moist climate, the redwoods reach over 300 feet high—as tall as a 30-story building. The trunks of redwood trees are often more than 10 feet in diameter, with the bark as thick as 12 inches. The redwood gets its name from the color of its wood, which turns from light to dark red as it weathers. Redwoods are sometimes called "California redwoods" or "coasts," since they grow along the Pacific coast of California.

The other true sequoia is the giant sequoia, which grows only on the western slopes of the Sierra Nevada Mountains of California. Once, the giant sequoias grew in many parts of the Northern Hemisphere. Today, they are found in only 70 groves high in the mountains at elevations of 5000 to 7800 feet. Although giant sequoias do not grow as tall as redwoods, their trunks are much larger. Some trunks are as large as 100 feet around the base.

The largest tree in the world is found in Sequoia National Park.

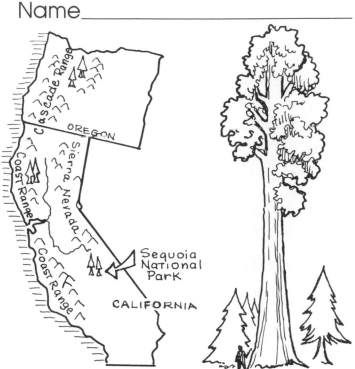

Name_____

Named the General Sherman Tree, it stands 272.4 feet high and measures 101.6 feet around its base. Scientists believe that this single tree could produce over 600,000 board feet of lumber!

The giant sequoia is classified as an evergreen tree. It grows scalelike needles up to ½ inch long and produces woody, oval-shaped cones about 2 to 3 inches long. Although lightning has destroyed the tops of many of the trees, they are considered to be among the hardiest of living things.

Scientists have dated many giant sequoias to be several thousand years old. The age is determined by counting the growth rings on a tree's trunk. Each growth ring stands for one year. Scientists have estimated that the General Sherman Tree is at least 3500 years old, and so it becomes not only the world's largest tree, but also one of the oldest living things on Earth.

• List ten events which have occurred during the life of the Sherman Tree.

The Sequoia

Name_____

Write, check.

The Sequoia is among the _____ and _____ of living things
   on Earth.

The Sequoia once grew ☐ only in extremely cold climates.
                      ☐ in forests over much of the world.

Today, Sequoias are found mainly in _____, where only
   ☐ two   ☐ five   kinds still grow:

_____.

The Redwood

. . .is the ☐ tallest ☐ widest   living tree.

. . .is found in the coastal mountains of northern _____ and

   southern _____ .

. . .grows to a height of _____ feet.

. . .often have trunks more than ☐10 ☐20   feet in diameter with the

   _____ as thick as 12 inches.

. . .gets its name from:

   ☐ the color of the leaves as they turn in the fall.

   ☐ the color of the wood, which turns from light to dark red as it weathers.

. . .are sometimes called "_____" or "_____."

The Giant Sequoia

. . .grows only on the western slopes of the _____

   Mountains of ☐ California. ☐ Oregon.

. . .once grew in many parts of the _____ Hemisphere.

. . .is found today in only ☐ 70 ☐ 7   groves high in the mountains at

   elevations of _____ to _____ feet.

The largest tree in the world

. . .is found in the _____ Park.

. . .is named _____ Tree.

. . .stands _____ feet high, and measures _____ feet around the base.

. . .is estimated to be ☐ at least 3500 years old.
                       ☐ a million years old.

Wonder About:

Niagara Falls

Niagara Falls is one of the most spectacular natural wonders of the world. The famous Falls are supplied by the Niagara River, which connects Lake Ontario and Lake Erie. The Niagara Falls, located midway in the river, pour 500,000 tons of water a minute into a deep gorge. The water drops in two sections divided by Goat Island. The right-hand section forms the American Falls, which is 193 feet high and over 1,000 feet wide. The left-hand section forms the Horseshoe Falls, which is 186 feet high and 2,100 feet wide.

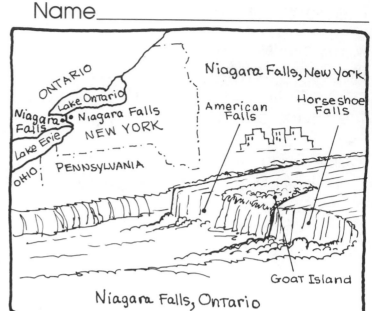

Niagara Falls, Ontario

Scientists believe that Niagara Falls was formed after the last ice sheet from the Ice Age had withdrawn from the area. The surface of the land had been changed by the ice. This caused waterways and streams to develop new paths. The result was an overflow of Lake Erie which produced Niagara Falls. Scientists believe the Falls are approximately 20,000 years old.

The Falls are formed over an outer layer of hard dolomitic limestone. This covers a softer layer of shale. The shale is more easily worn away which causes the harder limestone to form an overhanging edge. This allows the Falls to drop straight down at a sharp angle, which produces a spectacular sight. But through the years, the outer layer has broken off at times. This is causing the Falls to gradually move back up the river. This erosion is happening to the American Falls at the rate of 3 to 7 inches a year. But the edge of the Horseshoe Falls is being worn back at the rate of approximately three feet a year.

Through the years, Niagara Falls has been a tremendous attraction for sightseers. Observation towers and a special area, Cave of the Winds, **behind** the Falls, have allowed remarkable views. At night, the Falls are flooded with lights. A steamer, called the Maid of the Mist, takes visitors for a ride around the base of the Falls.

Niagara Falls has also irresistibly drawn daredevils who have wanted to test their courage. One such man, Charles Blondin, crossed the Falls on a tightrope in 1859. Four days later, he crossed again, only this time with a blindfold. A month later, he crossed for the third time carrying a man on his shoulders. And as if that weren't daring enough, he returned to cross the Falls once again—on stilts!

• Find out how Niagara Falls compares to Victoria Falls.

Write, circle, check.

Name_____

Niagara Falls is located midway in the _____ River, which connects Lake Placid Ontario and Lake ☐ Erie.
☐ Washington.

Check.

Scientists believe Niagara Falls was formed:

☐ as a result of a volcanic eruption.

☐ after the last ice sheet from the Ice Age had withdrawn.

The surface of the land had been changed by the ☐ sun.
☐ ice.
☐ falls.

Waterways and streams developed ☐ less water.
☐ new paths.

Write, check.

This caused an overflow of Lake _____, which produced Niagara Falls.

Scientists believe Niagara Falls to be approximately_____years old.

Niagara Falls flows over an outer layer of hard _____, which

covers a soft layer of ☐ mud.
☐ shale.

The constant flow of water over the land is gradually. . .

☐ eroding the land. ☐ causing a shortage of water.

The word **erosion** means:

☐ soil becomes rich with minerals from the water.

☐ the surface of the earth is worn away by the action of the water.

The land under the _____ Falls is eroding at a rate of 3 to 7 inches a year.

The land under the _____ Falls is eroding at a rate of approximately three feet a year.

True or False

_____ Niagara Falls is a tremendous attraction for sightseers.

_____ Visitors can only view the Falls from the bottom.

_____ At night, the Falls are flooded with lights.

_____ A plane, called The Maid of the Mist, flies visitors over the Falls.

_____ Visitors can view the Falls from "The Cave of the Winds."

_____ A daredevil crossed the Falls on a tightrope.

Wonder About:

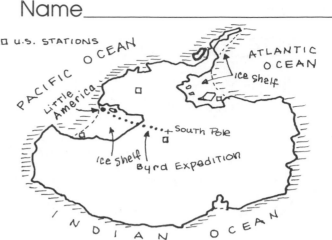

Antarctica

One of the most incredible natural wonders in the world is Antarctica, the continent surrounding the South Pole. It contains 90 percent of the world's ice. Antarctica, the coldest and most desolate region on Earth, covers 5,400,000 square miles. Much of the land is buried under snow and ice one mile thick. Mountains of ice, called glaciers, move slowly across the land to the sea. The winter temperatures reach −100°F in the interior of the continent. On the coast, the temperatures fall below −40°F. This frozen land lies over 600 miles from the tip of South America, the nearest land. New Zealand is 2,100 miles away and South Africa, 2,500 miles.

The interior of Antarctica is a frozen, lifeless region. The only animal life in Antarctica is found on the coastline or in the sea. Penguins, seals, whales and other fish and birds live in or close to the coastal waters. These animals all live on food from the sea.

The ancient Greeks called the North Pole, the Arctic. They believed that land at the South Pole must also exist. They called this supposed land, Antarctica, meaning the opposite of Arctic.

Through the centuries, hunters and whalers may have discovered this land. But in 1838, Lieutenant Charles Wilkes of the United States Navy, was sent to investigate this southern land. He reported back that the land was indeed large enough to be a continent. This opened up the way for explorers to study the region. But after several years, interest in Antarctica began to fade.

In 1928, Commander Richard E. Byrd of the U.S. Navy led a famous expedition to the South Pole. He and his men set up a base called Little America. On November 28, 1929, Byrd and his companions became the first men to fly over the South Pole. Until his death in 1957, Byrd took five expeditions to Antarctica. He helped establish scientific research bases and led the largest Antarctic expedition in history with over 4,000 men and 13 ships. The expedition was called Operation Highjump.

From July 1, 1957, to December 31, 1958, twelve nations joined together to explore and conduct research in Antarctica. The effort occurred during the International Geophysical Year (IGY). This effort involved over 10,000 men operating from over 40 research stations.

During IGY, the United States operated seven stations. Four of the stations have become permanent bases on Antarctica.

● Find three discoveries which were made in the Antarctica during the IGY.

Antarctica

. . . is the continent which surrounds the _____ Pole.

. . . contains ☐ 50 ☐ 90 percent of the world's ice.

. . . is the ☐ coldest ☐ largest and most desolate region on Earth.

. . . covers _____ square miles.

. . . has a _____-mile thick covering of snow and ice over much of its land.

. . . has a winter temperature of _____ F in the interior of the land.

. . . has a coastal temperature which falls below _____ F.

. . . lies over ☐ 6000 ☐ 600 miles from the tip of _____ America, the nearest land.

Write, check.

The ancient Greeks called the North Pole, the _____.

They believed that ☐ there must be land at the South Pole, too.
☐ there must be a West Pole.

The Greeks called this supposed land _____.

In 1838, Lieutenant _____ of the United States Navy was sent ☐ to Greece. ☐ to investigate Antarctica.

Write, check.

In 1928, Commander_____ of the United States Navy led an expedition to the South Pole.

Byrd and his crew. . .

. . . set up a base called _____.

. . . became the first men to fly over the _____, on November _____, 19 _____.

. . . made ☐ two ☐ five expeditions to Antarctica.

. . . led the largest expedition in history, called Operation _____, with over _____ men and _____ ships.

IGY stands for

I _____ G _____ Y_____ .

93

Wonder About:

Mount Everest

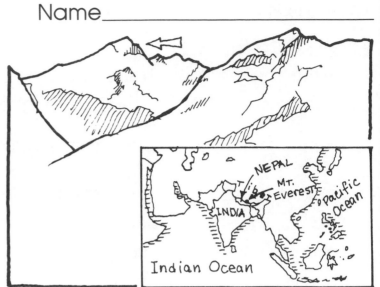

Mount Everest is one of the great natural wonders of the world. At 29,141 feet, it stands as the highest mountain in the world. Mount Everest is the highest peak in the Himalayas, a 1500 mile mountain range. Mount Everest can be seen from many parts of northeast India. It lies on the frontiers of Tibet and Nepal, north of India.

Mount Everest was named for Sir George Everest, a British surveyor-general of India. The people of Tibet call Mount Everest, Chomolungma. The people of Nepal call it Sagarmatha.

Through the years, many people tried to climb Mount Everest. The attempts were made hazardous by avalanches, crevasses, strong winds, extreme steepness and thin air. In 1922, seven climbers fell to their deaths on the slopes of the northeast ridge of Mount Everest, called the North Col. In 1924, George Mallory, England's greatest mountaineer, disappeared while trying to climb Mount Everest.

On March 10, 1953, an expedition of climbers left Katmandu, Nepal. They climbed the south side of the mountain, which had previously been called unclimbable. The climbers set up a series of camps as they advanced up the mountain. Few people were able to go to each new camp as they continued to climb. The last camp was formed at 27,900 feet by only two climbers. On May 29, 1953, the two climbers reached the top of Mount Everest. They were Sir Edmund Hillary of New Zealand, and Tenzing Norgay, a tribesman from Nepal.

In 1956, an expedition of climbers from Switzerland reached the summit of Mount Everest. They also were the first climbers to reach the top of Lhotse, the fourth highest peak in the world.

On May 1, 1963, James Whittaker became the first American to reach the top of Mount Everest. Other members of this expedition reached the top on May 22nd.

The ascent of Mount Everest became obtainable by the use of specialized clothing and gear designed to endure the extreme weather conditions. Also, oxygen equipment developed during World War II provided a defense against the thin air at high altitudes.

Mount Everest has been climbed by expeditions from England, Switzerland, America, Italy, China, Poland, India and Japan, among others.

• Find the name of the **second** highest mountain in the world.

Mount Everest

. . .is one of the great ☐ natural ☐ manmade   wonders of the world.

. . .stands _____ feet tall.

. . .is the ☐ coldest ☐ highest   mountain in the world.

. . .is the highest peak in the _____, a 1500 mile mountain range.

. . .can be seen from many parts of northeast _____.

. . .lies on the frontiers of _____ and _____ .

Write.

What are some of the hazards in mountain climbing?

_____   _____   _____

_____   _____

Check.

In 1922,   ☐ seven climbers fell to their deaths on Mount Everest.
           ☐ seven climbers reached the top of Mount Everest.

In 1924, England's greatest mountaineer,_____ , disappeared
   while climbing Mount Everest.

Match.

The people of Tibet. . .   . . .call Mount Everest, Sagarmatha.
The people of Nepal. . .   . . .call Mount Everest, Chomolungma.

Write 1-4.

◯ The climbers set up a series of camps as they advanced up the mountain.

◯ On May 29, 1953, the two climbers reached the top of Mount Everest.

◯ The last camp was formed at 27,900 feet by only two climbers.

◯ On March 10, 1953, an expedition of climbers left Katmandu, Nepal.

Write.

Name the first two climbers to reach the top of Mount Everest:

_____ of New Zealand and _____ , a
   tribesman from Nepal.

The first American to reach the top of Mount Everest was _____ .

Underline the sentences which tell what improvements aided climbers in their
attempts to climb Mount Everest.

Wonder About:

The Sahara

Stretching almost 3,000 miles across North Africa, the Sahara Desert is an incredible natural wonder of sand, rock and gravel. The Sahara covers over 3½ million square miles, which makes it by far the largest desert on Earth. It extends west to east from the Atlantic Ocean to the Red Sea.

The name Sahara comes from an Arabic word **Sahra**, which means desert. Because of the unusually low rainfall, even for a desert, the sun-scorched land and blistering winds make the Sahara the hottest region in the world during the summer. A sandy surface may reach a temperature of 170°F. The cloudless skies allow the daytime air temperature to reach 100°F. At night, the temperature often drops 40 to 50 degrees.

The Sahara's only vegetation is found near wells, springs or streams. These fertile areas are called **oases**. Some vegetation grows where the water table is close enough to the surface of the land to feed the roots of the plants. Throughout the desert are many dry stream beds, called **wadis**. During a rare rain, they will temporarily fill up with water.

The Sahara supports some animal life, too, such as camels, lizards and the addax, a desert antelope which carries a reserve of water in a sac within its body.

Some people of the Sahara live in tents which allows them to more easily move in search of grassy areas. These people, called Nomads, tend flocks of sheep, camels or goats. Others raise crops on land which has been irrigated.

Scientists believe that throughout the Ice Age, the Sahara was a rich grassland and hunting ground. Archeologists have recovered prehistoric relics which include stone tools and carvings of elephants, lions and giraffes. They believe that the Berbers, who live in northern Africa today, may be the descendents of the prehistoric people who once lived in that area. The Berbers are a tall, slender group of people with light skin and dark eyes and hair. They speak a language that resembles that of ancient Egypt. By the early ancient times, the Sahara was much as it is today.

Through the years, many plans to make the Sahara into fertile land again have not been successful. Some of these plans included digging artesian wells, or flooding areas with sea water from which the salt had been removed.

Today, the Sahara is being viewed as much more than a dry, hot desert. The discovery of rich oil and gas deposits underground have led to a modernization of transportation and the addition of pipelines to carry the oil hundreds of miles to the Mediterranean coast.

● Find out more about the Berbers and write a paragraph about them.

The Sahara

Name_____

. . . is the _____ desert on Earth.

. . . covers   north   to   east   from the _____ Ocean to the
              west   south

_____ Sea.

Underline.

In the summer, the Sahara . . .
    is the hottest region in the world.
    receives no rainfall.

Match, write, check.

40° to 50°F   the temperature of the sand's surface
100°F   the number of degrees the temperature can drop at night
170°F   the daytime temperature

The Sahara's only vegetation is found near

_____ , _____ or _____ .

These fertile areas are called ☐ wadis. ☐ oases.

The desert contains dry stream beds called _____ .

The desert supports some animal life such as:

_____ , _____ and _____ .

Match.

Nomads   Tent dwellers who roam the desert in search of grassy areas
Berbers   May be descendents of prehistoric dwellers of the area

True or False

_____ Scientists believe the Sahara was once covered with ice.

_____ Scientists believe the Sahara was once a rich grassland.

_____ Prehistoric relics have been recovered in the Sahara.

_____ Berbers speak a language much like the ancient Greeks.

Write.

What new discovery has been made in the Sahara in recent years? _____

_____

How has this discovery affected the Sahara? _____

_____

97

Wonder About:

The Amazon River

The Amazon River is called the greatest river system in the world. This natural wonder is 4,000 miles long and contains more water than the Mississippi, the Nile and the Yangtze rivers together. Although the Nile River is 200 miles longer, the Amazon River is more massive. It drains over 2,500,000 square miles of land before it empties into the Atlantic Ocean at a rate of three billion gallons of water a minute. The Amazon River is over 200 miles wide at its mouth.

The Amazon River begins as the Apurimac River high in the Andes Mountains of Peru in South America. As the small river flows, it is joined by waters from other rivers. The river continues to flow eastward through Brazil until it empties into the Atlantic Ocean.

Much of the Amazon River covers an area that makes up the world's largest tropical rain forest. The temperature in this region averages about 85° all year long. Rainfall ranges from 50–120 inches per year.

The Amazon River contains many varieties of fish, including the flesh-eating piranha and the pirarucu, one of the largest fish found in South America. The basin region of the Amazon contains creatures such as alligators, anacondas, parrots and thousands of unusual insects.

The first complete descent of the Amazon was made by an expedition led by Gonzalo Pizarro, in 1541.

Pizarro, a Spaniard, had sailed with Christopher Columbus on his discovery voyage to America. His expedition set out from the Andes with over 4,000 Indian slaves to search for the fabled city of El Dorado. One of the members of the expedition, Francisco de Orellana, left the group in the tropical rain forest as he went ahead looking for food and supplies. Orellana never went back, and eight months later he came to the mouth of the Amazon River.

In 1637, an expedition from Portugal explored the Amazon by traveling **up** the river to its source.

Almost three centuries later, the first scientific exploration of the Amazon was made by the Victorian naturalists, Alfred Wallace and Henry Bates.

Even though there is not a single bridge that crosses the Amazon River for its entire course, the Amazon basin has been opened to outsiders by other modern developments. The most important development is a series of landing strips cut into the thick jungles that link the isolated people to larger communities and cities through air transportation.

• Write how the planes have changed life for people living along the Amazon.

Write, check.

The Amazon River

. . .is the greatest _____ in the world.

. . .is ☐ 4,000 ☐ 40,000   miles long.

. . .contains more water than the _____, the _____,

    and the _____ Rivers together.

. . .is only surpassed in length by the _____ River.

. . .drains over_____ square miles of land.

. . .empties into the _____ Ocean at a rate of ☐ one

    ☐ three   billion gallons of water a minute.

. . .is over_____ miles wide at its mouth.

The Amazon River begins as the _____ River, high in the

    _____ Mountains of ☐ Peru ☐ Colombia   in South America.

The river flows ☐ westward ☐ eastward   through Brazil.

Much of the Amazon River. . .

    ☐ covers an area that makes up the world's largest tropical rainforest.

    ☐ covers an area of dry, barren desert.

The tropical rainforest averages _____ degrees, with _____ to _____
    inches of rainfall per year.

Name 2 kinds of fish found in the Amazon River.

_____   _____

Name 4 kinds of animals found in the basin region of the Amazon.

_____ _____ _____ _____

The word **expedition** means:

    ☐ a scientific laboratory.

    ☐ a journey for exploration.

The first complete descent of the Amazon River was made by an expedition

    led by _____ in 1541.

Pizarro had sailed with _____ on his discovery voyage to America.

One of the members of the expedition, _____, left the group to

    look for: ☐ food ☐ gold ☐ supplies

Orellana reached the mouth of the Amazon River_____ months later.

Underline the sentence that tells which expedition explored the Amazon by
traveling up the river.

Wonder About:

Easter Island

Few places in the world are more intriguing and mystifying than Easter Island, located in the Pacific Ocean 2,300 miles from the coast of Chile. Easter Island covers 63 square miles made up of rugged coastline and steep hills. Scientists believe the island began as a volcano. Three extinct volcanoes remain on the island, with the largest rising 1400 feet high.

On Easter Sunday of 1722, Dutch Admiral Jacob Roggevan and his crew landed on Easter Island aboard the Dutch ship Arena. The astonished crew found dozens of huge stone figures standing on long stone platforms. The statues, some measuring 40 feet tall, were similar in appearance. Their expressionless faces were without eyes. Huge red stone cylinders were placed on their heads. Since that time, the island has been a source of mystery and intrigue to scientists.

Archeologists believe that three different cultures lived on Easter Island. Around 400 A.D., the island was inhabited by a group of people who specialized in making small stone statues. Years later, another civilization tore down these statues and used them to build long temple platforms called ahus. These people carved more than 600 enormous stone busts of human forms and placed them on the ahus. Scientists believe that the statues were carved from hard volcanic rock in the crater walls of the volcano called Rana Roraka. The statues were chiseled with stone picks made of basalt. Although the statues weigh many tons each, it is believed that they were moved with ropes and rollers across the island and placed on the ahus. Some ahus still hold up to 15 statues!

About 1670, another group of people invaded the island. These invaders practiced cannibalism. During this time, many people began living in underground caves where they hid their treasures.

In 1862, almost the entire population of Easter Island was wiped out by a smallpox epidemic carried to the island by Peruvian slave hunters.

In 1868, missionaries came to Easter Island and introduced the inhabitants to Christianity.

Today, Easter Island is governed by Chile, a country of South America. Almost the entire population of 1600 people live in the small village of Hanga Roa on the west coast of the island.

• Write your own ideas about what the Easter Island statues stand for, and why they were built.

Easter Island

. . .is located in the _____ Ocean, 1500 2300 miles from the coast

of _____ .

. . .covers _____ square miles made up of:

☐ rugged coastline ☐ meadows ☐ steep hills ☐ waterfalls

. . .is believed to have begun as a _____ .

. . .contains ☐ twenty-three ☐ three extinct volcanoes, with the largest

rising _____ feet high.

The term "**extinct volcano**" means: ☐ inactive.
☐ extremely hot.

On _____ Sunday of 17____ , Dutch Admiral _____ landed

on Easter Island aboard the Dutch ship _____ .

Admiral Roggevan and his crew found:

☐ dozens of extinct animals.

☐ dozens of huge stone figures.

Write, underline.

Archeologists believe that _____ different cultures lived on Easter Island.
Around 400 A.D., Easter Island was inhabited by. . .
    a group of people who worshipped the sun.
    a group of people who specialized in making small stone statues.
Years later, Easter Island was inhabited by. . .
    a group of people who tore down the original statues.
    a group of people who painted the original statues.

Write, check.

These inhabitants

    built long temple platforms called _____ .

They carved more than _____ stone busts of ☐ humans
☐ animals

    from volcanic rock found in the volcano _____ .

Underline the sentence which tells how the statues were moved across the
island.

Match.

1862	Missionaries came to Easter Island.
1868	A smallpox epidemic killed many islanders.

       101

Answer Key

for
Reading Comprehension
Grades 5 – 6

Think About:

Ancient Babylonia

One of the oldest civilizations on Earth was located in an ancient region called Babylonia. This ancient civilization lasted over 2000 years. It was located around the Tigris and Euphrates Rivers in an area that is today called Iraq.

The Babylonian civilization centered around the ancient city of Babylon. Babylon, which means "gate of god", was the cultural, religious and trading center of Babylonia. The city was divided in half by the Euphrates River. Huge walls decorated with blue bricks and paintings of mythical beasts surrounded the city. Large bronze gates allowed people to enter and leave the city.

Babylon was a magnificent city. It contained many palaces and temples. The most famous was the temple of Bel Marduk, the patron god of Babylon. Inside the temple area stood the famous Tower of Babel. Located nearby were the Hanging Gardens of Babylon. The gardens were considered to be one of the Seven Wonders of the World. The gardens were grown on the roof of a large building. The roof was vaulted, or slanted. People used this as a

Name_____

shady, cool area to escape the heat.

The Babylonians worshipped thousands of gods. There were gods and goddesses for practically everything in their lives.

Many Babylonians were farmers. They learned to drain swamps, and more importantly, to irrigate land. They built a series of canals to carry water from the Tigris and Euphrates Rivers to the fields. Because of this, they were able to grow an abundance of vegetables, fruits and grains.

The Babylonians were excellent craftsmen. They learned to make sun-dried bricks which were painted and glazed to decorate buildings. They made elaborate carvings and statues and designed beautiful jewelry of silver and gold.

The Babylonians were one of the first civilizations to develop a system of writing. <u>They used this to record their history, literature, scientific studies and religious texts.</u>

The Babylonians were ruled by many great rulers. One ruler, Hammurabi, developed a set of laws for his people. Today, these famous laws are known as the Code of Hammurabi.

• From what you have read in the story, draw a picture showing how the city of Babylon may have looked.

Babylonia   **Name**_____

Write, circle.

One of the oldest civilizations on Earth was located in an ancient region called **Babylonia**.

The Babylonian civilization lasted over (2000)/5000 years.

Babylonia was located around the **Tigris** and **Euphrates** Rivers in an area that is today called China/(Iraq.)

The Babylonian civilization centered around the ancient city of **Babylon**.

Write, check, circle.

Babylon

. . .means " **gate** of **god** ".

. . .was the ☑cultural ☐dining center of Babylonia.
☑religious ☑trading

. . .was divided in half by the (Euphrates)/Tigris River.

. . .was surrounded by a wall decorated with (blue bricks)/jewels

and (paintings of kings and gods./paintings of mythical beasts)

Babylon contained many (palaces)/deserts and mountains./(temples)

The most famous was the temple of **Bel Marduk** the patron god of Babylon.

Inside the temple area stood the famous ☐statue of Venus.
☑Tower of Babel.

Located in Babylon was one of the **Seven** Wonders of the World.

It was called the **Hanging Gardens** of Babylon.

Underline the sentence that tells what the Babylonians used their system of writing to record.

Write, check.

One of the greatest rulers of Babylonia was **Hammurabi**.

Hammurabi developed a set of ☐temples
☑laws.

Today, these famous laws are known as the **Code** of **Hammurabi**.

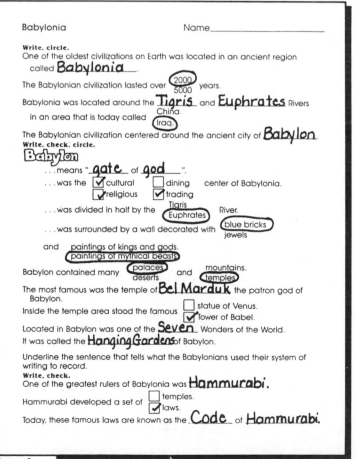

Page 2   Page 3

Answer Key

Page 4

Think About:
Ancient China

Name_____

The Chinese civilization is one of the oldest civilizations on Earth. It is believed to have begun over 4000 years ago.

The ancient Chinese were ruled by dynasties, a series of rulers from the same family.

The first known dynasty was the Shang Dynasty. Archeologists have found primitive writing on bones which tells of this culture, which existed over 3000 years ago. The Shang Dynasty was defeated by warriors from a new dynasty called the Chou.

The Chou Dynasty ruled China almost a thousand years. During this time, many local governments were formed throughout China. They fought constantly among themselves for power to rule certain parts, or provinces, of the country. The Chou Dynasty was replaced by the Ch'in Dynasty.

The Ch'in Dynasty broke down many of the local governments and set up one central government for the entire country. The Ch'in Dynasty was ruled by Shih Huang Ti, the first great Chinese dictator. He is famous for building the Great Wall of China, which still stands today. The Ch'in Dynasty was replaced by the Han Dynasty.

The Han Dynasty controlled China

for 400 years. During this time, Chinese culture developed rapidly. Art and sciences were valued and education was encouraged. After the Han Dynasty, China broke into many different warring states. This lasted for over 400 years.

Life in these ancient dynasties was different for each class of people. The Emperor lived in the capital city in splendid style. His home was a palace of many rooms, filled with gardens and courtyards.

The people were separated into groups, such as merchants, who sold or traded goods; artisans, who made tools and ornaments; and soldiers.

The peasants made up the largest group of people. They produced the food for the country. Their lives were simple and often, very hard. Most peasants lived in tiny, bare houses.

The ancient Chinese produced beautiful works of art. Ornaments and statues were often made of jade. Jade was called "the stone of heaven". The green stone was a symbol of wealth and power.

Painting became a popular art form during the Han Dynasty. Artists painted on wood, silk and paper.

Chinese musicians played instruments similar to our harp, flute and cymbals.

The ancient Chinese developed one of the earliest forms of writing. They first wrote on bones or bamboo. Later they made paper which was used to make books. The Chinese made the first dictionary over 2000 years ago!

• Draw a time line showing the dynasties of ancient China in the correct order.

Page 5

China   Name_____

Underline.
The Chinese civilization . . .
<u>is believed to have begun over 4000 years ago.</u>
is believed to have been ruled by 4000 rulers

Check.
The ancient Chinese were ruled by ☐ presidents ☑ dynasties.
The word **dynasty** means . . .
☐ a group of warriors.
☑ a series of rulers from the same family.

Write and check.
The first Chinese dynasty was the **Shang** Dynasty.
The Shang Dynasty . . .
☐ existed over 5000 years ago.
☑ is known because of primitive writing found on bones.
The Shang Dynasty was replaced by the **Chou** Dynasty.
The Chou Dynasty . . .
ruled China for almost a **1000** years.
ruled during a time of many ☐ princes
☑ local governments that
controlled ☐ dynasties of the country.
☑ provinces
The Chou Dynasty was replaced by the **Ch'in** Dynasty.
The Ch'in Dynasty . . .
☐ tore down the temples and built new ones.
☑ broke down the local governments and set up one central government for the entire country.
was ruled by the first great Chinese dictator, named **Shih Huang Ti**.
who was responsible for building ☑ the Great Wall of China.
☐ strong armies.

True or False
T The Chinese emperors lived in splendid style in castles.
F Most Chinese people lived in castles.
T The Chinese produced beautiful works of art.
F The Chinese called diamonds, "the stones of heaven".
T Jade was a symbol of wealth and power.
F The Chinese played instruments much like our piano.
T The Chinese developed one of the earliest forms of writing.

Page 6

Think About:
Ancient Egypt

Name_____

Ancient Egypt was one of the most fascinating civilizations in history. The ancient Egyptians were a creative and intelligent people.

Ancient Egypt was located along the Nile River. Most of the land in that area was dry and sandy, which made farming difficult. But the soil along the Nile River was black and rich. Egyptian farmers were able to grow crops in this rich soil.

Egyptians wore light clothing because the climate was so warm. Both men and women wore make-up. Egyptian art shows that they especially used black lines of make-up around their eyes. Many Egyptians wore rings, bracelets, beads and wide jeweled collars. It was common for Egyptians to dye their hair with henna, a red dye.

The Egyptians spoke a language made of several other languages. No one knows how their language sounded. They developed a way of writing their language in picture symbols called hieroglyphics. Hieroglyphic carvings on tombs and monuments have been recovered from ancient ruins by archeologists.

Most of the Egyptians built their cities along the Nile River. The most famous cities of ancient Egypt were Memphis and Thebes.

Memphis was the first capital of Egyptian government. Later, the capital was moved to Thebes. The Egyptians had a sacred burial ground near Thebes called the Valley of the Tombs of the Kings.

The ancient Egyptians were very religious. They believed that they would go to another life after death. To prepare for that life, many rulers, called pharaohs, had huge tombs built and filled with great riches, food and clothing. The Egyptian pyramids are the most famous burial tombs from ancient Egypt. Perhaps the most famous discovery of modern times was the tomb of King Tutankhamon, which was discovered in the Valley of the Tombs of the Kings in 1922.

The civilization of ancient Egypt lasted about 2,500 years before it was conquered by invading armies. Historians believe that Egypt was conquered because it could not defend itself against armies which fought with iron weapons. Much of the civilized world had developed sources of iron. This period was known as the Iron Age. Without iron weapons, Egyptian armies were unable to defend their country.

• Find out when, how and by whom the Egyptian civilization was conquered.

Page 7

Egypt   Name_____

Write and check.
Ancient **Egypt** was built along the ☑ Nile ☐ Amazon River.

Match.
Most soil in Egypt . . . ⟍ was rich and black.
The soil along the Nile . . . ⟋ was dry and sandy.

Write and check.
The ancient Egyptians
. . . wore **light** clothing, because the climate was so warm.
. . . wore **make-up**, especially around their eyes.
. . . wore ☑ rings ☑ bracelets
☐ crowns ☐ bonnets
☑ beads ☑ jeweled collars
. . . often dyed their hair red with **henna**.

The ancient Egyptians wrote in picture symbols, called **hieroglyphics**.

The two most famous cities of ancient Egypt were **Memphis** and **Thebes**.

Rulers in Egypt were called **pharaohs**.

Ancient

1→ E g y p t
2→ l i g h t
5→ hieroglyphics
3→ make-up
9→ Tutankhamon
6→ Memphis
8→ pharaohs
4→ henna
7→ Thebes

True or False
T The ancient Egyptians were very religious.
T The ancient Egyptians believed in life after death.
F The ancient Egyptians built tombs as extra rooms in which to keep their possessions.
T The pharaohs built tombs and filled them with riches to take to the next life.
F The pyramids were built for soldiers to live in.
T The pyramids are the most famous burial tombs from ancient Egypt.

Write.
One of the greatest discoveries of modern times was the tomb of King **Tutankhamon**.

Answer Key

Page 8

Think About:
Ancient Greece

Name_____

Ancient Greece was one of the most important civilizations in history. It existed over 2000 years ago.

The ancient Greeks developed democracy, a way of life that allowed the people to take part in their own government. This form of government was much different from other cultures of that time, which were ruled by kings and emperors.

Ancient Greece had two main cities, Sparta and Athens.

Life in Sparta emphasized physical activities. Young boys were trained in gymnastics and other sports. Although most Spartans grew into strong adults, they were usually uneducated. Very few Spartans could read or write.

Life in Athens was much different from life in Sparta. The Athenians believed in developing the mind as well as the body. They learned mathematics, literature, writing and music, as well as gymnastics. Individuals were encouraged to develop their own talents. Athens became the center of Greek culture.

The ancient Greeks lived simply. They built their homes of stone and brick around open courtyards.

The Greeks ate only two meals a day. The morning meal was called ariston. It consisted of beans or peas. The night meal, called deipnon, was a large meal of cheese, olives, bread and meat.

The Greek men and women wore cloaks and sandals.

The people of ancient Greece worshipped many different gods. The chief god, Zeus, was believed to live on Mount Olympus. Zeus was considered the ruler of all other gods and goddesses, such as: Apollo, god of light and youth; Poseidon, god of the sea; Athena, goddess of war and wisdom; and Aphrodite, goddess of love and beauty. Many Greek myths and legends were written about their gods and goddesses.

The Greeks built many temples for their gods and goddesses. One of the most famous temples was the Parthenon, the temple of Athena. Today, parts of it still stand in Athens on a hill known as the Acropolis.

Each year, the Greeks celebrated festivals in honor of their gods. One festival gathered people from all over Greece for a contest of running and throwing. The festival was called the Olympic Games!

- Write a paragraph telling how life in Sparta and Athens differed. Tell which city you would have wanted to live in, and why.

Page 9

Greece   Name_____

Underline.
The word democracy means . . .
   a way of life that encourages people to exercise.
   <u>a way of life that allows people to take part in their own government.</u>

Ancient Greece had two main cities: **Sparta** (A) **Athens** (B)

Write A or B.

B Believed in developing the mind as well as the body

A Emphasized physical activities

A Young boys were trained in gymnastics and other sports.

B Individuals were encouraged to develop their own talents.

A Most citizens grew into strong adults.

B They learned mathematics, literature, writing and music, as well as gymnastics.

A Very few people could read or write.

B The city became the center of Greek culture.

Check, write, circle.

The ancient Greeks

. . . built homes of ☑ stone and brick ☐ wood around open **courtyards.**

. . . worshipped ☑ many ☐ twelve gods.

. . . wore (hoods) (cloaks) and (sandals) boots.

. . . ate only (one) ~~two~~ meals a day, called: **ariston** (morning) and **deipnon** (night)

Write.

Gods and Goddesses . . . Who were they?

Aphrodite goddess of love and beauty

Zeus_____ ruler of all other gods and goddesses

Apollo_____ god of light and youth

Athena_____ goddess of war and wisdom

Poseidon_____ god of the sea

Zeus was believed to live on **Mount Olympus.**

The **Parthenon** was the temple of Athena.

The Parthenon still stands in the city of **Athens**

Page 10

Think About:
Ancient Rome

Name_____

Ancient Rome was a powerful civilization which began almost 3000 years ago.

No one knows exactly how Rome was founded. Legend says that twin brothers, Romulus and Remus, were the founders of Rome. The legend says that the twin boys were cast into the Tiber River as babies. They were saved by a she-wolf, who raised them. As young men, they built a city on the spot where the wolf had pulled them from the river. The city was Rome.

The lives of the ancient Romans centered around the forum, an open marketplace where public meetings were held. Many of the Roman rulers built their own forums. Today, ruins of these forums still stand, including the forum of the great Roman emperor, Julius Caesar.

The Romans lived in houses which consisted of one large four-sided room called an atrium. Wealthy Romans added many more rooms around their atriums. Some homes even had piped-in water.

The Ancient Romans ate three meals a day. Their breakfast was

usually bread and honey. For lunch they ate meat and fruit. Dinner was their largest meal, often served as a banquet. It included eggs, fish, meat, vegetables and fruit. In place of butter, the Romans used olive oil. Instead of sugar, they used honey.

The Romans wore a garment called a tunica. A tunica had short sleeves and hung to the knees. Tunicas were worn by both men and women. The men wore a draped cloth, called a toga, over the tunica.

The Romans worshipped many gods, such as Juno, Mars and Jupiter. The Romans later adopted some of the Greek gods and goddesses and gave them new names. For example, the Greek goddess Aphrodite became the Roman goddess, Venus.

The ancient Romans were very interested in law and government. They established principles of law that are still used today. One principle was called equity. <u>It meant that a law should be flexible enough to fit different circumstances.</u>

The ancient Romans were famous for their many festivals which were usually held in the huge open theater called the Colosseum. There they watched gladiators either fight each other or wild beasts.

One of the most popular events was the chariot races held in a large arena called a circus. The largest circus in ancient Rome was called the Circus Maximus, which held 180,000 Roman spectators.

- Write an example of a situation today in which the principle of equity would be important.

Page 11

Rome   Name_____

Write 1-5. How was Rome Founded?

Legend says . . .

① Twin baby boys, Romulus and Remus, were cast into the Tiber River.

④ Romulus and Remus built a city on the spot where they were saved.

③ Romulus and Remus were raised by the she-wolf.

⑤ The city was called Rome.

② The baby boys were pulled from the river by a she-wolf.

Underline, check.
The forum . . .
   was a one room house that people lived in.
   <u>was an open marketplace where public meetings were held.</u>

Many Roman rulers ☑ built their own forums. ☐ burned forums.

Circle, match, write.
The ancient Romans ate (three) ~~four~~ meals a day.

breakfast ⟍ meat and fruit
lunch ⤬ eggs, fish, meat, vegetables and fruit
dinner ⟋ bread and honey

In place of sugar, the Romans used **honey**.

In place of butter, the Romans used **olive oil**.

Check.
The Romans lived in one large four-sided room called:
☐ lodge ☑ an atrium ☐ a great room

True or False

The ancient Romans . . .

T adopted some of the Greek gods and goddesses.

F used the Greek names for their gods and goddesses.

T established principles of law.

T held festivals in the open theater called the Colosseum.

F watched chariot races in the forum.

T watched chariot races in an arena called a circus.

The largest circus in Rome was called the

Circus Maximus, which held **180,000** spectators.

Underline the sentence which explains the meaning of equity, a principle of law.

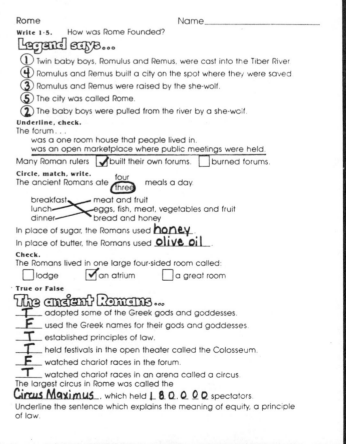

Answer Key

Page 12

Think About:

The Decathlon

The decathlon is one of the most famous contests in sports. Decathlon is a Greek word which means "ten contests". The first decathlon was added to the Olympic Games in 1912. It was added in honor of athletes who competed in the original Olympic Games in Greece. Most of the games in the early Olympics were contests of running, jumping and throwing. Today, these kinds of events are called track and field events.

A decathlon is a two-day contest that features ten separate events in track and field. The events for the first day are the 100-meter dash, long jump, shot-put, high jump and the 400-meter run. The events for the second day are the 110-meter hurdles, discus throw, pole vault, javelin throw and the 1500-meter run.

The 100-meter dash starts the decathlon. It takes just seconds for the athletes to run the 100-meter race, which is approximately the length of a football field.

An athlete has three chances for a high score in the long jump and high jump events. The best score out of three attempts is used.

The shot-put is an event that requires a tremendous amount of power to throw a 16-pound metal ball, called a shot, as far as possible.

The final event of the first day is the 400-meter run. This race is almost a quarter of a mile in length. It is a hard race to run because it is too long to run in one burst of energy. But

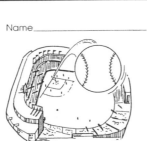

it is too short to run at a slower pace. Some people have called this the "murderous race".

The second day begins with the 110-meter hurdles. The runners must not only run fast, but also jump over ten hurdles which are 3½ feet tall.

The discus throw is an event in which an athlete throws a four-pound metal plate, called a discus, as far as possible.

The pole vault is one of the hardest events of the decathlon. An athlete runs and lifts himself high into the air on a pole. The aim is to jump over a high bar without knocking it down.

The javelin throw event requires an athlete to throw a javelin, a kind of spear, as far as possible.

The final event is the 1500-meter race, which is just a little less than a mile in distance.

The goal of every decathlon athlete is to win the gold medal in the Olympic games. The winner is often called, "the world's greatest athlete".

• Find the names of three Olympic Decathlon winners.

Page 13

The Decathlon   Name_____

True or False

The Decathlon...

__T__ is one of the most famous contests in sports.

__F__ is a Greek word that means "no contest".

__T__ was added to the Olympic Games in 1912.

__F__ was added to the Olympic Games in honor of the Greek god. Zeus.

__T__ was added to the Olympic games in honor of the athletes who competed in the original Olympic Games.

__T__ is a Greek word that means "ten contests".

Write.
Name the five events for each day of the decathlon.

First day
100-meter dash
long jump
shot-put
high jump
400-meter run

Second Day
110-meter hurdles
discus throw
pole vault
javelin throw
1500-meter run

Write the name of the event (or events) by each sentence.

__discus throw__ An athlete throws a four-pound metal plate as far as possible.

__100 meter dash__ This race is approximately the length of a football field. It takes just seconds to run.

__pole vault__ An athlete jumps over a high bar by using a pole to lift himself into the air.

__high jump__ An athlete has three chances for a high score.

__1500 m. run__ The final event of the second day. The race is a little less than a mile.

__shot-put__ An athlete throws a 16-pound metal ball as far as possible.

__110-meter hurdles__ While running, an athlete jumps over ten hurdles which are 3½ feet tall.

__javelin throw__ An athlete throws a "spear" as far as possible.

__400-meter run__ The final event of the first day. This race is called "the murderous race".

Page 14

Think About:

The World Series

Every year baseball takes center stage for one of the world's most famous sporting events—the World Series. The World Series is a series of baseball games which decide the world championship of baseball.

The World Series matches the American League champion team against the National League champion team. The first team to win four games out of seven wins the World Series.

The World Series was first played in 1903. The American League champions, the Boston Pilgrims, played the National League champions, the Pittsburgh Pirates. This first World Series was won by the Boston Pilgrims, now named the Boston Red Sox.

Although the World Series seemed off to a great start in 1903, the next year was a different story. In 1904, the New York Giants refused to play the Boston Pilgrims in the World Series. To this day, no one is sure why they refused, but 1904 was to be the only year in World Series history which did not have a world championship series.

For a team to make it to the World Series takes months of hard work and

a lot of talent. Most teams play over 150 games between April and October of each year. At the end of the regular season, the two best teams from each league play in the World Series.

Through the years, many great baseball players, such as; <u>Babe Ruth</u>, <u>Jackie Robinson</u>, <u>Joe Di Maggio</u> and <u>Lou Gehrig</u>, have played in the World Series.

Some performances are hard to forget, such as Reggie Jackson's three straight home runs in the last game of the 1977 World Series.

Many World Series records have been broken through the years. But one record which has never been broken was set in 1956 by a little-known player named Don Larsen, who pitched a no-hitter game for the New York Yankees.

• Find the names of the last two teams to play in the World Series.

Write.

The __World Series__ decides the championship of baseball.
The World Series is played between the champions of the __American__
League and __National__ League.

Page 15

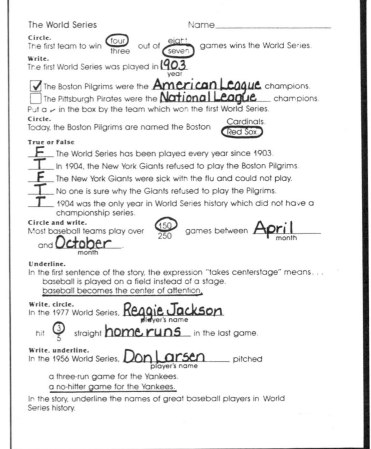

The World Series   Name_____

Circle.
The first team to win (four) three out of eight (seven) games wins the World Series.

Write.
The first World Series was played in __1903__
                                          year

☑ The Boston Pilgrims were the __American League__ champions.

☐ The Pittsburgh Pirates were the __National League__ champions.

Put a ✓ in the box by the team which won the first World Series.

Circle.
Today, the Boston Pilgrims are named the Boston   Cardinals. (Red Sox)

True or False

__F__ The World Series has been played every year since 1903.

__T__ In 1904, the New York Giants refused to play the Boston Pilgrims.

__F__ The New York Giants were sick with the flu and could not play.

__T__ No one is sure why the Giants refused to play the Pilgrims.

__T__ 1904 was the only year in World Series history which did not have a championship series.

Circle and write.
Most baseball teams play over (150) 250 games between __April__ month
and __October__ .
           month

Underline.
In the first sentence of the story, the expression "takes centerstage" means. . .
baseball is played on a field instead of a stage.
<u>baseball becomes the center of attention.</u>

Write, circle.
In the 1977 World Series, __Reggie Jackson__
                           player's name
hit (3) 5 straight __home runs__ in the last game.

Write, underline.
In the 1956 World Series, __Don Larsen__ pitched
                          player's name
a three-run game for the Yankees.
<u>a no-hitter game for the Yankees.</u>

In the story, underline the names of great baseball players in World Series history.

Answer Key

Page 16

Think About:

Name_____

Stanley Cup

Today, one of the most popular spectator sports in the world is ice hockey. Each year, the teams of the National Hockey League play a series of games to determine the championship of ice hockey. The winner is presented an award called the Stanley Cup. The Stanley Cup is one of the most prestigious awards in the world of sports.

Ice hockey is now an international sport. But nowhere is hockey more popular than in Canada. Over 125 years ago, hockey-on-ice was played in Montreal, Canada. In 1870, the first official rules of the game were written. By 1880, official teams were organized into leagues. Some of those first games were played on town ice rinks which had bandstands right in the middle of the rinks! Later, special ice hockey rinks were built which even featured lights hung from telegraph poles.

The popularity of the game seemed to sweep through Canada. One of hockey's greatest fans was Lord Stanley of Preston, the sixth Governor General of Canada. Lord Stanley organized a championship game in which Canadian ice hockey

teams would compete. On March 22, 1894, the first Stanley Cup game was played in Montreal, Canada, at Victoria Rink. <u>The championship game received its name from the award presented to the winner.</u> Donated by Lord Stanley, the first award was a sterling silver cup.

After that first championship game in 1894, the game of ice hockey continued to grow in popularity. Today, the National Hockey League includes teams from America as well as Canada. And each year, the teams play a series of games to determine who wins the championship of ice hockey and the Stanley Cup.

- Find out how many teams in the National Hockey League are Canadian and how many are American.

Write.
The _Stanley Cup_ is the award presented to the championship team in ice hockey.

Circle.
Ice hockey was played in (Montreal, Canada) over (125) ~~200~~ years ago.
~~London,~~

Page 17

The Stanley Cup

Name_____

True or False.

Ice Hockey...

__F__ is played each year in the Stanley Sports Center.

__T__ teams of the National League play a series of games for the championship.

__T__ is now an international sport.

__F__ was probably first played in France.

__T__ is probably most popular in Canada.

Underline.
Some of the first games . . .
were played on <u>indoor ice rinks in Montreal.</u>
were played on <u>town ice rinks which had bandstands.</u>
Later, special ice hockey rinks were built . . .
<u>which featured lights hung from telegraph poles.</u>
which were named after each hockey team.

Write.
One of ice hockey's greatest fans was **Lord Stanley** of Preston.

Check.
Lord Stanley was ☐ the mayor of Montreal, Canada.
☑ the sixth Governor General of Canada.

Circle.
Lord Stanley organized a (championship) game in which (Canadian) ice
charity American
hockey teams would compete.

Write.
When was the first Stanley Cup game played? **March 22, 18 94**
In what city was the first Stanley Cup game played?
Montreal Canada
At what rink was the first Stanley Cup game played? **Victoria Rink**.
Underline the sentence that tells how the Stanley Cup game got its name.

Check.
The word prestigious means: ☑ honored and important.
☐ cautious and careful.

Page 18

Think About:

Name_____

Leonardo da Vinci

Leonardo da Vinci was one of the greatest artists of all time. He is remembered not only as a painter, but also as a sculptor, musician, inventor, astronomer, scientist and engineer.

Leonardo was born in 1452, in Vinci, Italy. As a young boy, he showed a talent for mathematics and painting. His father took him to Florence, Italy, to study painting and engineering. Florence was a city where many well-known artists lived. Leonardo became well-known in Florence as a gifted young painter. Soon he was painting better than his teachers. In 1472, at the age of twenty, Leonardo was asked to join the painter's guild in Florence. This was an honor for Leonardo to be officially accepted by so many other great artists.

When Leonardo was thirty years old, he decided to move to Milan, Italy. He began working for the Duke of Milan, who wanted to make Milan a beautiful and famous city like Florence.

While in Milan, Leonardo painted one of the most famous paintings in history—"The Last Supper".

"The Last Supper" was painted on the wall of a small church near the duke's castle. People came from many countries to see the painting. The King of France liked the painting so much that he wanted to move the

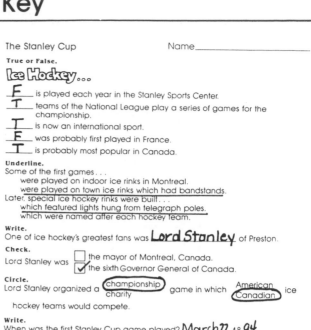

parachute

flying machine

entire church back to France. Today, the painting is still found on the wall of the little church in Italy.

In 1499, Leonardo returned to Florence. Here he painted his other famous painting, the "Mona Lisa". The "Mona Lisa" was a painting of a twenty-four year old wife of a wealthy merchant. Her name was Lisa del Gioconda. The painting is famous for Lisa's mysterious smile. For centuries, people have wondered what her smile really meant.

Leonardo is remembered for other contributions, such as sketch designs for flying machines long before anyone ever believed man could fly. Leonardo also drew detailed sketches of the human body and how it worked. He wrote thousands of pages of notes on mathematics and science. Sometimes he even wrote his notes backwards and read them with a mirror!

Many of Leonardo's sketches and notes have been used through the years to help scientists and inventors make new discoveries.

- Write your name and address backwards. Use a mirror to read them.

Page 19

Leonardo da Vinci

Name_____

Write.
Leonardo is remembered not only as a painter, but also a:
sculptor **musician** **inventor**
astronomer **scientist** **engineer**

True or False

__T__ As a young boy, Leonardo showed a talent for mathematics and painting.

__F__ Leonardo's father took him to Rome, Italy, to study painting and engineering.

__T__ Florence was a city where many well-known artists lived.

__T__ Leonardo became well-known in Florence as a gifted young painter.

__F__ Leonardo became dissatisfied and stopped painting.

__T__ Leonardo was soon painting better than his teachers.

__T__ In 1472, Leonardo was asked to join the painter's guild in Florence.

Write.
When Leonardo was thirty, he moved to **Milan**, Italy.

Write and underline.
There he worked for the **Duke** of **Milan**, who wanted to . . .
make Leonardo a famous painter.
<u>make Milan a beautiful and famous city like Florence.</u>

While in Milan, Leonardo painted one of the most famous paintings in history, called **"The Last Supper"**.

Check, circle, write.
"The Last Supper" . . .
☑ was painted on the wall of a small church.
☑ was so famous that people came from other countries to see it.
☐ was moved to Rome, Italy, in 1650.
☑ is still found on the wall of the little church in Italy.

In 1499, Leonardo returned to (Florence).
Vienna.

In Florence, he painted a portrait of the wife of a wealthy merchant. The painting is called the **Mona Lisa**. The lady in the painting was named **Lisa del Gioconda**.

The painting is famous for: ☐ its unusual colors.
☑ Lisa's mysterious smile.

Answer Key

Page 20

Think About:

Raphael

Name_____

Raphael was one of the greatest artists in history. He was born in Urbino, Italy, in 1483. Raphael's father was a painter. He encouraged Raphael to begin painting at an early age. As a young man, Raphael was sent to study with Peruginoi, a master painter of the day. Peruginoi became a great influence on Raphael's style of painting. Before long, he was painting better than his teacher.

Raphael's work attracted the attention of a wealthy merchant, Angelo Doni, who hired Raphael to paint for him. He painted many portraits and religious scenes. These paintings made him wealthy.

In 1504, Raphael traveled to Florence, where he studied painting for four years. It was during this time that he painted "The Entombment", one of his most famous paintings. It was also during this time that he painted many of the Madonnas, for which he is so famous.

In 1508, Raphael returned to Urbino. He was hired to paint for the Duke of Urbino. The duke asked for a group of paintings that told the story of St. George. St. George was a legendary hero who lived in ancient times. According to the legend, St. George slew a terrible dragon and saved the King's daughter. These paintings made Raphael even more respected as an artist.

This same year, Raphael left for Rome. At the same time, Michelangelo, another great painter in Rome, was painting the ceiling of the Sistine Chapel.

During this time in Rome, Raphael painted the masterpieces for which he is most famous. He became so popular that he could hardly finish all the work he was hired to do. Whenever he left his house, he was surrounded by admirers. Young painters followed him hoping to learn from him. He was called the "Divine Raphael". Raphael's last great work, the "Transfiguration" was completed by one of his pupils.

In 1514, Raphael was made chief architect of St. Paul's Church in Rome. He painted many beautiful madonnas during this time.

In 1520, Raphael became ill and died. His death saddened all of Rome.

- Find out more about the legendary St. George. Write a story of his adventure.

Page 21

Raphael...

Name_____

T was one of the greatest artists in history.
F was born in Urbino, Italy, in 1483
T was the son of a doctor.
T was encouraged by his father to begin painting at an early age.
F was sent to study painting with Michelangelo.
T was sent to study painting with Peruginoi.
T became a better painter than his teacher.

Write, circle.
A wealthy merchant, _Angelo Doni_, hired Raphael to paint for him.
Raphael's paintings made him (wealthy) / unhappy.

In 1504, Raphael moved to _Florence_ where he studied painting for ten / (four) years.

Write.
During this time . . .
Raphael painted his famous painting, "_The Entombment_".
Raphael painted many of the _Madonnas_, for which he is so famous.

In 1508, Raphael returned to _Urbino_ where he was hired to paint for the _Duke_ of _Urbino_
The duke asked Raphael for a group of paintings that told the story of St. _George_

Underline.
St. George . . .
<u>was a legendary hero who lived in ancient times.</u>
was the King of Urbino who lived in ancient times.

Check.
While in Rome . . .
☑ Raphael painted many masterpieces.
☑ Raphael became extremely popular as a painter.
☐ Raphael painted the ceiling of the Sistine Chapel.

Write.
Raphael was called the "_Divine Raphael_".

Page 22

Think About:

Rembrandt

Name_____

Rembrandt was one of the greatest artists of all time. He was born on July 15, 1606, in Leiden, Holland. Rembrandt began painting at an early age. At the age of fifteen, he traveled to Amsterdam to study art. But he soon returned home to paint on his own.

Rembrandt's first paintings were of subjects from the Bible and from history. He used bright colors and glossy paints. These paintings were very popular, and soon, Rembrandt was well-known in his community.

In 1628, Rembrandt began to teach art. He was a respected teacher with many students.

In 1632, Rembrandt again moved to Amsterdam. He began painting portraits of many well-known people in Amsterdam. He soon became famous in Holland for his beautiful portraits.

In 1634, he married a wealthy and educated girl named Saskia. They moved into a large home where Rembrandt hung many of the paintings that he had collected.

Rembrandt continued to succeed as an artist. But tragedy began to strike his family. Three of his four children died at a very early age. And then in 1642, his wife, Saskia, died.

Rembrandt became very sad. He began to paint with darker colors. But, somehow, his painting grew even more beautiful. <u>He used dark colors around the figures in his paintings. The figures themselves were painted as if a soft light were shining on them.</u> Rembrandt began to paint more for himself and less for other people. Although his work was brilliant, he was not able to make enough money to keep his house. In 1657, his house and his possessions were auctioned off. Rembrandt was bankrupt.

But until he died on October 4, 1669, Rembrandt continued to paint. His most famous painting was named "The Night Watch".

Rembrandt created over 600 paintings, 300 etchings and 1400 drawings. Some of his most fascinating paintings were the portraits which he painted of himself. The hundred self-portraits leave a remarkable record of his lifetime.

- Draw a self-portrait.

Check.
Rembrandt's first paintings were of subjects from the
☐ legends   ☑ history.
☑ Bible   ☐ myths.
and from

Page 23

Rembrandt...

Name_____

T was one of the greatest artists of all time.
F was born on July 15, 1606, in Florence, Italy.
T began painting at an early age.
T traveled to Amsterdam at the age of fifteen to study art.
F stayed in Amsterdam for thirteen years.

Check and write.
Rembrandt used ☐ soft / ☑ bright colors and _glossy_ paints.

Underline.
In 1634, Rembrandt married . . .
<u>a wealthy and educated girl named Saskia.</u>
a poor girl from Amsterdam named Saskia.

Check, write.
Although Rembrandt was successful as an artist,
☑ tragedy ☐ good fortune began to strike his family.

Three of his _4_ children died at a very early age.
In 1642, ☐ Rembrandt's father died.
☑ Rembrandt's wife died.
Rembrandt's sadness caused him to use ☑ darker ☐ lighter colors.

Underline.
In 1657 . . .
Rembrandt sold his house and moved to Italy.
<u>Rembrandt's house and possessions were auctioned off.</u>

Check, circle, write.
Rembrandt was ☑ bankrupt. ☐ retired.
Rembrandt died on October 4, (1669) / 1700.
Rembrandt's more famous painting was named "_The Night Watch_"

Rembrandt's other works included:
☐ paintings   ☑ drawings
☑ etchings   ☑ self-portraits

Underline the sentences which describe how Rembrandt used dark and light colors to help "spotlight" the figure he was painting.

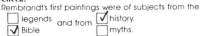

Answer Key

Page 24

Think About:
Vincent Van Gogh

Name_____

Vincent Van Gogh is remembered as one of the greatest painters of modern art. It is hard to believe that the life of one of the world's most famous painters was filled with so much loneliness and disappointment.

Vincent Van Gogh was born in Zundert, Holland, in 1853. Most of his young manhood was spent trying to find a suitable career that he could succeed in. At the age of sixteen, he left home to live with an uncle who was an art dealer. Vincent was not successful, and he soon left. He had not enjoyed being a businessman. He wanted to be a minister.

At the age of twenty-five, Van Gogh became a preacher in a poor mining town in Belgium. He was so concerned for the poor that he went without food so that he could give more to the poor. But some church officials did not approve of Vincent's behavior. He was released from his duties as a minister.

By 1880, Van Gogh had decided to become a painter. In his early years as a painter, he completed "The Potato Eaters", one of his finest paintings. He chose dark gray and brown colors to paint the poor Dutch peasants eating dinner after working hard through the day.

In 1886, Van Gogh moved to Paris to be near his brother, Theo, who was a great admirer of Van Gogh's work.

In 1888, Van Gogh moved once again. This time he traveled to Arles in France. It was here that Van Gogh's style of painting began to change. Before, he had used many dark, even drab colors in his painting. But now, he began painting with bright, intense colors, such as red and yellow. His painting, "Sunflowers", was an example of how his work had changed. Van Gogh also began using a flat knife, instead of a brush, to apply thick paint in heavy strokes.

Van Gogh was painting more than he had ever painted before. In the last five years of his life, he painted more than *eight hundred* paintings! Many painters have not completed that many paintings in a lifetime!

But Van Gogh was becoming a troubled man. He also began suffering from seizures. During one seizure, he cut off his ear. Van Gogh died in July, 1890.

Van Gogh sold only one painting during his lifetime. He received no praise for his work. Only after his death was his work recognized for its greatness. One of the greatest painters of all time died thinking that he was a failure!

• Fine the names of three more famous paintings by Van Gogh.

Page 24

Page 25

Vincent Van Gogh   Name_____

Check.
Vincent Van Gogh . . .
- [✓] is remembered as one of the greatest painters of modern art.
- [✓] had a life filled with much loneliness and disappointment.
- [ ] had a life filled with excitement and adventure.

Circle, write.
Vincent Van Gogh was born in (1853) in **Zundert** Holland.

At the age of twenty-five, Van Gogh became a **preacher** in a poor mining town in (Belgium).

Circle, write, check.
By 1880, Van Gogh had decided to become a teacher. (painter).

One of his finest paintings, **"The Potato Eaters"**, showed Dutch peasants eating dinner after working hard through the day.

He painted with dark yellow and (brown) (gray) green colors.

In 1888, Van Gogh moved to Arles, **France**.

Van Gogh's style of painting
- [✓] began to change.
- [ ] stayed the same.

He began painting with [ ] dull [✓] bright and intense colors, such as **red** and yellow.

An example of his new style was the painting, **"Sunflowers."**

Van Gogh painted with a [ ] brush. [✓] flat knife.

Check, write, circle.
Van Gogh
- . . . began to suffer from [✓] seizures. [ ] tuberculosis.
- . . . painted more than **eight hundred** paintings in the last (five) ten years of his life.
- . . . sold [ ] only eight [✓] only one painting during his lifetime.
- . . . received [✓] no praise [ ] much praise for his work during his lifetime.
- . . . died in July, **1890**.
- . . . died thinking he was a **failure**.

Page 25

Page 26

Think About:

Johann Sebastian Bach

Name_____

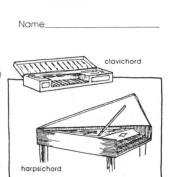

clavichord

harpsichord

Johann Sebastian Bach is known as one of the greatest musicians of all time. Bach was born on March 21, 1685, in Germany. Bach's family was famous in Germany because of their music. Many of Bach's aunts, uncles, cousins, brothers and sisters sang or played musical instruments. Bach's father taught him to play the violin at an early age.

When Bach was only ten years old, his mother and father died. Bach went to live with an older brother. Bach's brother taught him to play the harpsichord and the clavichord, which were forerunners of the piano.

Bach also began to play the organ. This became his favorite instrument. Sometimes he would walk over a hundred miles to hear the music of Remken, the greatest organist of the time.

Bach was becoming more and more interested in music. He began composing music. He became famous as an organist and a composer.

One day he was asked to compete in a harpsichord contest. The contest was held in the court of King Ferdinand Augustus. Bach was to compete with a famous French musician, named Marchand. On the day of the contest, Marchand left Germany. Many said he was afraid to perform with the great Bach. Bach played so well that he was asked to stay as a court musician.

By this time, Bach was married and had seven children. But in 1720, his wife, Maria, died. Bach later married again and had thirteen more children.

Bach spent his later years as a director of music for a large school. Here, he continued to compose music. His compositions were famous for their style, called baroque.

Baroque music is lively—it is played in constant motion. Today, Bach is called the "genius of baroque music".

Bach's twenty children became musicians. Two sons, C.P.E. Bach and Johann Christian Bach became well-known as composers. But neither became as famous as their father, Johann Sebastian Bach, who is remembered today as "The Father of Modern Music".

• Write about Bach's children that became famous composers.

Page 26

Page 27

Circle, write, check.
Johann Sebastian **Bach**
- . . . was one of the greatest (musicians) artists of all time.
- . . . was born on March 21, 1685, in **Germany** .
- . . . was born into a family of well-known artists (musicians) .
- . . . was taught to play the [ ] piano [✓] violin by his father.
- . . . was **10** years old when his parents died.

After the death of his parents, Bach went to live
- [ ] with his grandparents. [ ] by himself. [✓] with an older brother.

Write.
Bach's brother taught him to play the **harpsichord** and the **clavichord** .

Both instruments were forerunners of the **piano** .

Check.
Bach also began to play the [✓] organ. [ ] french horn.

Underline.
Sometimes Bach . . .
   would perform for the great organist, Remken.
   <u>would walk over a hundred miles to hear the great organist, Remken.</u>

Check.
Soon, Bach became famous as . . .
- [ ] a teacher. [✓] a composer.
- [✓] an organist. [ ] an author.

Circle, write, check.
Bach was asked to compete in a (harpsicord) organ contest, held in the court of King **Ferdinand Augustus**

Bach was to compete with the famous [ ] German [✓] French musician, named **Marchand**.

On the day of the contest, Bach (Marchand) left Germany.

Underline.
Many said that Marchand . . .
   was ill and unable to perform in the contest.
   <u>was afraid to perform with the great Bach.</u>

Write.
Bach played so well that he was asked to stay as a **court musician**

Page 27

Answer Key

Page 28

Think About:

Wolfgang Amadeus Mozart

Name_____

Wolfgang Amadeus Mozart was known as the "Wonder Child", who later became one of the greatest composers of all time.

Mozart was born on January 27, 1756, in Austria. When he was just three years old, he learned to play the harpsicord. By the time he was five years old, he was composing music. At the age of six, he was invited to perform for the Empress of Austria. Mozart astonished people with his musical ability. He was called a child genius.

Mozart's father, Leopold, was a well-known musician. He was very proud of his son. Leopold took Mozart on tours through Europe. Mozart performed for kings and queens, other musicians and in churches.

In 1781, Mozart left his home town and traveled to Vienna, Austria. He married the next year. Mozart did not have a regular job. He earned a living by selling the music which he wrote. He also gave music lessons and performed his music in public.

Mozart continued to compose music. His compositions included operas, symphonies, concertos, serenades and church music.

Mozart wrote twenty-two operas. Today many of his operas are still famous, such as: "The Marriage of Figaro", "Don Giovanni" and "The Magic Flute". The first two are written in Italian. The last is written in German. Today, "Don Giovanni" is considered the world's greatest opera!

Mozart wrote at least forty symphonies for orchestras. His most famous symphony is nicknamed "The Jupiter".

He wrote special music for orchestras, called serenades. A serenade was a softer, lighter kind of music. Many serenades were written to be performed outdoors. One of his most famous serenades is called "A Little Night Music".

Mozart also composed music to be played with the orchestra playing in the background. Sometimes Mozart would perform these solos himself.

Mozart wrote many compositions for churches. His most famous work is called "Requiem". "Requiem" was a mass, or prayers, for the dead. He wrote part of "Requiem" while he was dying of an illness.

Mozart was only thirty-five years old when he died. He died a poor man on December 5, 1791.

Today, Mozart is considered to have been a musical genius. His music is known throughout the world.

- Find and write the story of the opera, "Don Giovanni".

Page 29

Wolfgang Amadeus Mozart

Name_____

Write.
Wolfgang Amadeus Mozart was known as the "__Wonder Child__".

Circle and write.
Mozart was born on January 27, (1756) / 1854, in __Austria__

Match.
three years old —— Mozart began composing music.
five years old —— Mozart performed for the Empress of Austria.
six years old —— Mozart learned to play the harpsicord.

True or False
T - Mozart was called a child genius.
F - Mozart's father, Leopold, was a well-known artist.
T - Leopold took Mozart on tours through Europe.
T - Mozart performed for kings and queens.
F - In 1781, Mozart left home and traveled to England.
T - In Vienna, Mozart made a living by selling his music and giving music lessons.
T - Mozart married the year after moving to Vienna.

Write, circle.
Mozart's compositions included: __operas__, symphonies, __concertos__, __serenades__ and __church music__.

Mozart wrote ~~12~~ (22) operas. Three of his most famous operas are:
"__The Marriage of Figaro__" "__Don Giovanni__" X
"__The Magic Flute__"
Put an X beside the opera considered to be the world's greatest opera

Circle, write, check.
Mozart wrote at least ~~four~~ (forty) symphonies for __orchestras__
His most famous symphony is nicknamed the "__The Jupiter__"
Mozart wrote special music for orchestras called (serenades). [operas]
A serenade was a ☑ softer ☐ faster music written to be performed __outdoors__
☑ lighter
One of Mozart's most famous serenades is called "__A Little Night Music__"

Page 30

Think About:

Frederic Chopin

Name_____

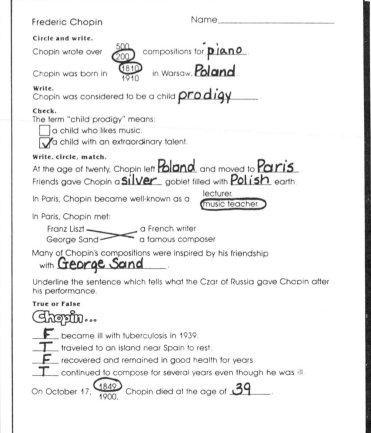

Frederic Chopin was one of the most brilliant composers for piano in history. During his life, Chopin wrote over 200 compositions for piano.

Chopin was born on February 22, 1810, in Warsaw, Poland. He began to take piano lessons at age six. By the time he was eight, he was performing in public. At the age of twelve, he was composing his own music. Chopin was considered to be a child prodigy—a child with an extraordinary talent.

For several years, Chopin traveled through the country performing his music. At one concert, the Czar of Russia was so thrilled with Chopin's music that he gave him a diamond and gold ring. Although Chopin enjoyed performing for large groups, he preferred playing for small groups in the homes of friends.

When Chopin was twenty years old, he left Poland and moved to Paris, France. When he left his home, friends gave him a silver goblet filled with Polish earth. Chopin kept this gift for the rest of his life.

Chopin's music was very popular in Paris. He became a well-known music teacher. It was while living in Paris that Chopin met two very important people in his life. One was Franz Liszt, another famous composer. Liszt and Chopin became friends and

shared their love of music.

It was Liszt who introduced Chopin to a woman named George Sand, a French writer. Sand and Chopin became dear friends. Many of his most famous compositions were inspired by their friendship.

In 1839, Chopin became ill with tuberculosis. Although he traveled to an island near Spain to rest, his condition worsened. Chopin somehow managed to continue to compose and perform his music for several years.

On October 17, 1849, Chopin died at the age of 39. Chopin's own music was played at his funeral. The Polish earth, which Chopin had brought from Poland almost twenty years before, was sprinkled on his grave.

- Find the names of three of Chopin's compositions.

Underline.
Frederic Chopin. . .
was one of the most brilliant composers for violin in history.
was one of the most brilliant composers for piano in history.

Page 31

Frederic Chopin

Name_____

Circle and write.
Chopin wrote over ~~500~~ (200) compositions for __piano__

Chopin was born in (1810) / 1910 in Warsaw, __Poland__

Write.
Chopin was considered to be a child __prodigy__

Check.
The term "child prodigy" means:
☐ a child who likes music.
☑ a child with an extraordinary talent.

Write, circle, match.
At the age of twenty, Chopin left __Poland__ and moved to __Paris__
Friends gave Chopin a __silver__ goblet filled with __Polish__ earth.
In Paris, Chopin became well-known as a [music teacher]. [lecturer]

In Paris, Chopin met:
Franz Liszt —— a French writer
George Sand —— a famous composer

Many of Chopin's compositions were inspired by his friendship with __George Sand__.

Underline the sentence which tells what the Czar of Russia gave Chopin after his performance.

True or False
(Chopin)...
F - became ill with tuberculosis in 1939.
T - traveled to an island near Spain to rest.
F - recovered and remained in good health for years.
T - continued to compose for several years even though he was ill.

On October 17, (1849) / 1900, Chopin died at the age of __39__.

Answer Key

Page 32

Think About:

Peter Tchaikovsky

Name_____

Peter Tchaikovsky composed some of the most beautiful music ever written for orchestras.

Tchaikovsky was born in Russia on May 7, 1840. His father and mother began piano lessons for him at an early age.

When Tchaikovsky was eleven, he was sent to a special school to study law. For several years he did not have time to think about his music. But at the age of twenty-two, he once again began to study music at the St. Petersburg Conservatory. Four years later, he became a teacher at the Moscow Conservatory of Music.

While teaching, Tchaikovsky began to compose. But with his teaching duties, it was hard to find the time he needed to write music. An important event took place which solved this problem. A rich admirer gave Tchaikovsky enough money to quit his teaching job and spend all his time writing music. Tchaikovsky never met this admirer in person, but they exchanged letters for years.

Over the next fourteen years, until his death on November 6, 1893, Tchaikovsky wrote some of the most beautiful compositions ever written.

Tchaikovsky wrote beautiful symphonies, concertos and operas. But his best known work may be his

three ballets: "Swan Lake", "Sleeping Beauty" and the "Nutcracker".

The "Nutcracker" tells the story of a little girl's dream. On Christmas night, she dreams that one of her gifts, a nutcracker, comes to life and battles an army of soldiers led by the Mouse King. In her dream, the nutcracker turns into a prince and carries her off to the Sugar Plum Kingdom. The ballet features a Russian Dance, Chinese Dance, Arab Dance, Dance of the Flutes and the Waltz of the Flowers.

Many of the melodies from the "Nutcracker", "Swan Lake" and other works are well-known today. That is why Tchaikovsky is often called the "Master of the Medley".

Tchaikovsky traveled to many countries, including America. In 1891, he went to New York City to take part in the opening of Carnegie Hall.

• Find and write the story of the ballet, "Swan Lake".

Underline.

Peter Tchaikovsky...

__composed some of the most beautiful music ever written for orchestras.__

composed some of the most beautiful music ever written for the organ.

Page 32

Page 33

Peter Tchaikovsky   Name_____

Write, circle, check.

Tchaikovsky was born in **Russia** on May 7, ~~1940~~ (1840).

His father and mother began ☐ violin ☑ piano lessons for him at an early age.

When Tchaikovsky was eleven, he was sent to a special school to study **law**.

At the age of twenty-two, Tchaikovsky began to study ~~law~~ (music) at the **St. Petersburg Conservatory.**

Four years later, Tchaikovsky became a teacher at the **Moscow Conservatory** of **Music**.

True or False

T While teaching, Tchaikovsky began to compose music.

F Tchaikovsky had plenty of time for composing his music.

T It was difficult for Tchaikovsky to find time for composing.

T A rich admirer gave Tchaikovsky money to quit teaching and spend his time composing music.

F Tchaikovsky met his admirer only once.

T Tchaikovsky never met his admirer in person, but they exchanged letters for years.

Circle and write.

Tchaikovsky's best known work may be his three ~~waltzes~~ (ballets)

"**SwanLake**", "**Sleeping Beauty**" and the "**Nutcracker.**"

Underline.

The **Nutcracker** tells the story of...

a little girl's trip to the magic Christmas Village.

__a little girl's dream on Christmas night.__

Write, check, circle.

The little girl dreams that one of her gifts, a **nutcracker**

☑ comes to life and battles an army of soldiers.

☐ comes to life and teaches her to waltz.

The soldiers are led by the **Mouse King**

The nutcracker turns into a ~~king~~ (prince) and carries her off to the

Sugar Plum Kingdom.

Page 33

Page 34

Think About:

The Typewriter

Name_____

It might truly be said that the typewriter was one small invention that made a big difference. To understand how big the difference was, try to imagine what it was like when businesses had to write everything by hand. __Every letter, every report, every bill, every memo—all had to be written by hand.__

In the early 1800's, many inventors tried to make a machine that would take the place of so much handwriting. In 1867, an American, Christopher Sholes, decided to build a writing machine. His first experimental machine printed one letter—W. Sholes began working with two other inventors, Carlos Gliddon and Samuel Soule. In 1868, these three men designed the first typewriter. Their invention had 11 keys which typed only capital letters. Sholes continued to improve the invention. In 1874, a company put the typewriter on the market. Soon, other companies were producing typewriters. By the early 1900's, portable typewriters were being sold. In the 1920's, electric typewriters were on the market.

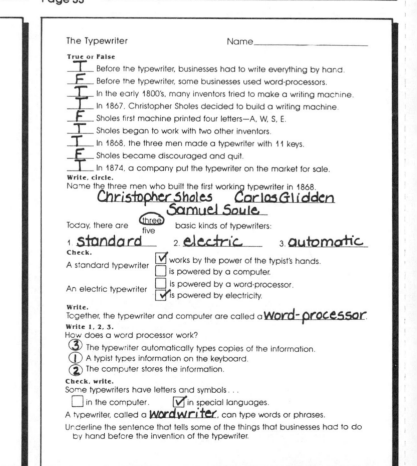

Today, there are 3 basic kinds of typewriters: standard, electric and automatic.

A standard typewriter works by power of the typist's hands. An electric typewriter is powered by electricity. Although the typist must still press the keys, the operation is much easier and faster than the standard typewriter.

An automatic typewriter has an electric typewriter keyboard connected to a computer. Together, the typewriter and the computer are called a word-processor. When a typist types on the keyboard, the computer stores the information. Then, the typewriter automatically types copies of the information.

Typewriters are made in several thousands of keyboard styles. Many electric typewriters have the letters and symbols on a ball which can be easily removed to change the style of type.

Special typewriters have letters and symbols in different languages. A typewriter, called a wordwriter, can type entire words, or even phrases, with a single touch of a key. Today, typewriters are continuing to change and advance with the Computer Age.

• Write a list of the ways you will use a typewriter in your future.

Page 34

Page 35

The Typewriter   Name_____

True or False

T Before the typewriter, businesses had to write everything by hand.

F Before the typewriter, some businesses used word-processors.

T In the early 1800's, many inventors tried to make a writing machine.

T In 1867, Christopher Sholes decided to build a writing machine.

F Sholes first machine printed four letters—A, W, S, E.

T Sholes began to work with two other inventors.

T In 1868, the three men made a typewriter with 11 keys.

F Sholes became discouraged and quit.

T In 1874, a company put the typewriter on the market for sale.

Write, circle.

Name the three men who built the first working typewriter in 1868.

Christopher Sholes   Carlos Glidden   Samuel Soule

Today, there are (three) ~~five~~ basic kinds of typewriters:

1. **standard**   2. **electric**   3. **automatic**

Check.

A standard typewriter ☑ works by the power of the typist's hands.
☐ is powered by a computer.

An electric typewriter ☐ is powered by a word-processor.
☑ is powered by electricity.

Write.

Together, the typewriter and computer are called a **word-processor**

Write 1, 2, 3.

How does a word processor work?

③ The typewriter automatically types copies of the information.

① A typist types information on the keyboard.

② The computer stores the information.

Check, write.

Some typewriters have letters and symbols...

☐ in the computer.   ☑ in special languages.

A typewriter, called a **wordwriter**, can type words or phrases.

Underline the sentence that tells some of the things that businesses had to do by hand before the invention of the typewriter.

Page 35

Answer Key

Page 36

Think About:
The Telescope

Name_____

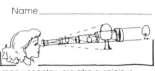

The invention of the telescope opened up outer space for observation and study. Before the telescope, people could only guess about the stars, planets and other heavenly bodies. The only knowledge of space was gathered by what people could see with the naked eye. With the invention of the telescope, it was possible to discover, study and even photograph outer space.

Many people believe that the telescope was invented by Galileo, the great Italian astronomer. But most historians believe that a Dutch optician, named Hans Lippershey, made the first telescope in 1608. He was not allowed to have a patent for his invention.

Galileo heard of Lippershey's invention and the following year, 1609, he built his own telescope. Galileo's telescope magnified heavenly bodies 33 times larger than they appear to the naked eye. Galileo made some amazing discoveries with his telescope. He discovered the rings around the planet Saturn. He discovered that the moon has mountains and valleys; until then the moon was believed to have a smooth surface. Perhaps Galileo's greatest discovery was that four moons orbit the planet Jupiter. He called these moons the Medician stars. The name came from the Medici family which ruled Galileo's home province in Italy.

Galileo's discoveries created a sensation. He became famous, but many people were also suspicious and frightened by his discoveries.

Today, discoveries in space are still being made almost daily using telescopes of much greater strength.

One of the simplest kinds of telescopes is the refracting telescope, made with a long tube. One end of the tube contains two lenses called the eyepiece and ocular. They are used to magnify the image to be seen. The other end of the tube contains the objective lens, which gathers the light from the object to be seen. When light rays strike the objective lens, they bend and gather at one spot called the focal point. The eyepiece takes the light rays, or image, at the focal point and magnifies that image.

Another kind of telescope is called the reflecting telescope. Sir Issac Newton built one of the first reflecting telescopes. Instead of glass lenses in the objective, it uses mirrors. The reflecting telescope is used to see objects that are at greater distances because it can gather more light than a refracting telescope.

There are other more advanced telescopes being developed today. Because of telescopes, the science of astronomy is possible. With new and better telescopes, we will learn even more about our universe.

• Draw a picture showing the discoveries which were made by Galileo through his telescope.

Page 37

The Telescope   Name_____

Check.
Before the telescope, people . . .
- [✓] could only guess about many of the stars and planets
- [ ] thought that there were rings around the moon
- [✓] gained their knowledge of space by what could be seen with the naked eye

The term "naked eye" means . . .
- [ ] seeing something for the first time.
- [✓] seeing without the aid of magnification.

True or False

_T_ Lippershey was not allowed to have a patent for his invention.

_T_ Galileo built his own telescope in 1609.

_F_ Galileo built the first telescope in history.

_T_ Galileo's telescope magnified heavenly bodies 33 times.

_F_ Galileo was unable to discover anything new in space.

What were Galileo's amazing discoveries?
__rings around Saturn; mountains & valley on the moon; 4 moons orbit Jupiter__

Write.
Name two kinds of telescopes:
__refracting__ (A)   __reflecting__ (B)

Write A, B.

_B_ Sir Issac Newton built one of the first ones.

_A_ One of the simplest kinds of telescopes

_B_ Uses a mirror in the objective, instead of glass

_A_ Bends light rays to form a focal point

_B_ Used to see objects that are at a greater distance

Write 1, 2, 3, 4.
How does a refracting telescope work?

_2_ The objective lens bends the light rays.

_4_ The eyepiece takes the light rays at the focal point and magnifies that image.

_1_ The objective lens gathers light from the object to be seen.

_3_ The bent light rays form a focal point.

Page 38

Think About:
The Hot-Air Balloon

Name_____

For thousands of years, people have been fascinated with the idea of flying. The idea was especially appealing to two French brothers, Jacques and Joseph Montogolfier. In the late 1700's, they began experimenting with the idea of a hot-air balloon.

Their first experiment was to fill small paper bags with smoke. They found that the bags would rise in the air. The Montgolfiers first believed that the smoke made the bags rise. But later, they realized that it was the hot air, and not the smoke itself, that caused the bags to rise.

The Montgolfier brothers continued to experiment. In 1783, they put a hot-air balloon in the air for eight minutes. The balloon carried a rooster, a sheep and a duck! They landed safely after history's first real balloon flight.

The next month, a French scientist, Jean de Rozier, became the first person to fly in a hot-air balloon. The balloon was made by the Montgolfier brothers. The balloon rose over 300 feet into the air. The flight lasted 25 minutes as de Rozier floated over Paris, France.

About the same time that the Montgolfier brothers were making their hot-air balloons, another Frenchman, named Jacques Charles, was making a balloon that was filled with hydrogen, a gas which is lighter than air.

In December of 1783, Charles made the first flight in a hydrogen

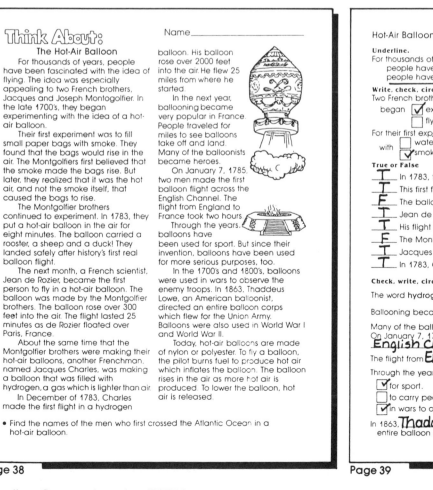

balloon. His balloon rose over 2000 feet into the air. He flew 25 miles from where he started.

In the next year, ballooning became very popular in France. People traveled for miles to see balloons take off and land. Many of the balloonists became heroes.

On January 7, 1785, two men made the first balloon flight across the English Channel. The flight from England to France took two hours.

Through the years, balloons have been used for sport. But since their invention, balloons have been used for more serious purposes, too.

In the 1700's and 1800's, balloons were used in wars to observe the enemy troops. In 1863, Thaddeus Lowe, an American balloonist, directed an entire balloon corps which flew for the Union Army. Balloons were also used in World War I and World War II.

Today, hot-air balloons are made of nylon or polyester. To fly a balloon, the pilot burns fuel to produce hot air which inflates the balloon. The balloon rises in the air as more hot air is produced. To lower the balloon, hot air is released.

• Find the names of the men who first crossed the Atlantic Ocean in a hot-air balloon.

Page 39

Hot-Air Balloons   Name_____

Underline.
For thousands of years . . .
    people have used hot-air balloons to fly across the country.
    <u>people have been fascinated with the idea of flying.</u>

Write, check, circle.
Two French brothers __Jacques__ and __Joseph Montogolfier__
    began [✓] experimenting with the idea of a hot-air balloon.
        [ ] flying hot-air balloons for the French government.
For their first experiment, the brothers filled __small paper bags__
    with [ ] water.
         [✓] smoke.   The (hot air) / smoke caused the bags to rise in the air

True or False

_T_ In 1783, the Montgolfier brothers put a hot-air balloon in the air.

_F_ This first flight lasted eight minutes.

_F_ The balloon carried a dog, mule and duck.

_T_ Jean de Rozier was the first person to ride in a hot-air balloon.

_T_ His flight lasted 25 minutes as he floated over Paris.

_F_ The Montgolfiers' balloons were filled with hydrogen.

_T_ Jacques Charles made a balloon filled with hydrogen.

_T_ In 1783, Charles made the first flight in a hydrogen balloon.

Check, write, circle.

The word hydrogen means:
    [ ] air that is extremely hot.
    [✓] a gas that is lighter than air.
Ballooning became very popular in [ ] Italy. [✓] France.
Many of the balloonists were treated as __heroes__.
On January 7, 1785, two men made the first flight across the __English Channel__.
The flight from __England__ to __France__ took (two) / twelve hours.
Through the years, balloons have been used . . .
    [✓] for sport.
    [ ] to carry people to work each day.
    [✓] in wars to observe enemy troops.

In 1863, __Thaddeus Lowe__, an American balloonist, directed an entire balloon corps for the Union Army.

Answer Key

Page 40

Think About:
The Television

Name_____

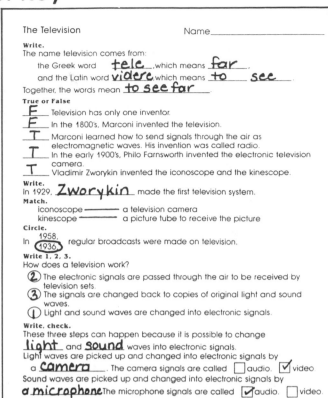

The invention of the television changed the world in many important ways. Television has given people the opportunity to see and hear people, places and events from around the world. Television has become one of the world's most important forms of communication. The word "television" comes from the Greek word "tele", which means far, and the Latin word "videre", which means to see. Together, the words mean to see far.

Television does not have just one inventor. In the 1800's, an Italian inventor named Marconi discovered how to send signals through the air as electromagnetic waves. His invention was the radio. This set the stage for the invention of television. In the early 1900's, a young American, Philo Farnsworth, began experimenting with an idea to send pictures as well as sound through the air. This idea resulted in the invention of the electronic television camera.

About the same time, an American scientist, Vladimir Zworykin, invented the iconoscope and the kinescope. The iconoscope was a television camera. The kinescope was a picture tube to receive and show the picture. In 1929, Zworykin made the first television system.

It wasn't until 1936 that regular broadcasts were made on television.

But how does a television work? The picture that you see on a television set comes from 3 basic steps. First, light and sound waves are changed into electronic signals. The light and sound waves come from the scene that is being televised. Next, these electronic signals are passed through the air to be received by individual television sets. Last, these signals are unscrambled and changed back into copies of the original light and sound waves to be seen and heard on a television set. In this way a picture is "moved" from the original scene to your television set.

These three steps can happen because it is possible to change light and sound waves into electronic signals. The light waves are picked up and changed into electronic signals by a camera. The sound waves are picked up and changed into electronic signals by a microphone. The camera signals are called video; the microphone signals are called audio.

To produce the electronic signals in color, certain color signals are added to the video. Three primary colors of light; red, blue and green, are used to produce television pictures in color.

Most electronic signals are carried through the air. Other means, such as microwaves, cable and satellites are also used to carry television signals.

• Write a paragraph telling how television can be used to educate people.

Page 41

The Television

Name_____

Write.
The name television comes from:
the Greek word **tele** ,which means **far** ,
and the Latin word **videre** which means **to** **see** .
Together, the words mean **to see far**

True or False
- **F** Television has only one inventor.
- **F** In the 1800's, Marconi invented the television.
- **T** Marconi learned how to send signals through the air as electromagnetic waves. His invention was called radio.
- **T** In the early 1900's, Philo Farnsworth invented the electronic television camera.
- **T** Vladimir Zworykin invented the iconoscope and the kinescope.

Write.
In 1929, **Zworykin** made the first television system.

Match.
iconoscope ——— a television camera
kinescope ——— a picture tube to receive the picture

Circle.
In 1958, / **1936** regular broadcasts were made on television.

Write 1, 2, 3.
How does a television work?
- **2** The electronic signals are passed through the air to be received by television sets.
- **3** The signals are changed back to copies of original light and sound waves.
- **1** Light and sound waves are changed into electronic signals.

Write, check.
These three steps can happen because it is possible to change **light** and **sound** waves into electronic signals.
Light waves are picked up and changed into electronic signals by a **camera** . The camera signals are called ☐ audio. ☑ video
Sound waves are picked up and changed into electronic signals by **a microphone** The microphone signals are called ☑ audio. ☐ video.
To produce electronic signals in color, three **primary** colors of light are used to produce all colors. The three primary colors of light are:
red , **blue** and **green** .

Page 42

Think About:

Name_____

The Jet Engine

The invention of the jet engine in the 1930's caused a dramatic change in flying. Before jet engines were used, airplanes were driven by propellers. With the power of jet engines, airplanes were suddenly able to fly at amazing new speeds. Jet engines have made it possible for some planes to fly fast enough to break the sound barrier!

Jet engines are built on a principle called jet propulsion. Jet propulsion works much like a balloon that is blown up and then turned loose to fly around as its air escapes. A jet engine sucks in air and mixes it with fuel. The air-fuel mixture burns and creates pressure inside, like a full balloon. The burned gases come out of the engine like the air does as you release a balloon. The engine reacts to this release of pressure by moving forward, as the deflating balloon does.

The forward motion of a jet engine is called thrust. The burned gases that come out are called jet exhaust.

There are several main kinds of jets: turbojets, pulsejets, ramjets and rockets.

A turbojet is a jet engine which is used in most passenger airplanes. It is much smaller, but more powerful and faster than a propeller engine.

A pulsejet is lighter and simpler than a turbojet. Pulsejets were used in World War II to power missiles.

A ramjet is the simplest of all engines. This engine works best at speeds faster than sound.

A rocket does not use the air around it like other jet engines. It carries its own oxygen needed to burn the fuel. Rockets can work in outer

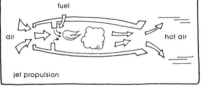

fuel
air
hot air
jet propulsion

space and can fly at very high speeds.

Jet engine airplanes can fly higher and faster than propeller-driven airplanes. Almost all airplanes today are jet powered.

Although real jet engines were first built in the 1930's, the first jet engine was actually designed over 2000 years ago in Egypt. The Chinese used rockets to frighten enemies in 1230. In each century after 1230, people designed or made jet engines. But it wasn't until the mid-1900's that people began to understand how to actually put jet power to use.

• Find the name of the famous person who first broke the sound barrier.

Write.
Jet engines are built on a principle called **jet propulsion**

Page 43

The Jet Engine

Name_____

True or False
- **T** The invention of the jet engine caused a dramatic change in flying.
- **F** Jet planes were first flown in 1912.
- **T** Before jet planes, airplanes were driven by propellers.
- **T** Because of jet engines, airplanes could fly much faster.
- **F** Propeller planes can fly fast enough to break the sound barrier.
- **T** Some jet planes can fly fast enough to break the sound barrier.

Write 1, 2, 3, 4.
How does jet propulsion work?
- **2** The air-fuel mixture burns and creates pressure.
- **4** The engine reacts to this release of pressure by moving forward.
- **1** A jet engine sucks in air and mixes it with fuel.
- **3** The burned gases come out of the engine.

Match.
thrust ⤬ burned gases which are released from a plane
jet exhaust forward motion of a jet engine

Write, check, circle.
Name four kinds of jets:
turbojets **pulsejets** **ramjets** **rockets**

A turbojet engine is used in most ☐ propeller ☑ passenger airplanes.

A turbojet engine is ☑ smaller ☑ faster than a propeller engine.
☐ larger ☑ more powerful

A pulsejet is lighter and simpler than a **turbojet** .

Pulsejets ☐ were used in World War II propeller planes.
☑ were used in World War II to power missiles.

A **ramjet** is the simplest of all jet engines.

A ramjet works best at speeds **faster** / slower than sound.

A rocket **does** / **does not** use the air around it, like other jet engines.

A rocket carries its own **oxygen** needed to burn the fuel.

Jet engines were actually designed over **2000** years ago in **Egypt**

Answer Key

Page 44

Think About:
The Space Shuttle

fuel tank
orbiter
rocket boosters
USA

Name_____

The invention of the Space Shuttle has been a major advancement in space travel. Before the Space Shuttle, rockets which were used to launch spaceships and satellites were not used again.

This one-time launching was not only expensive, it also required too much time to prepare a new craft for use.

The Space Shuttle system, which began to operate in the early 1980's, works as a launch vehicle with a big difference. A Space Shuttle can be used again and again. This means that the Space Shuttle greatly reduces the cost of launching flights into space. Without the Space Shuttle system, plans to build spacelabs or space stations would be far too expensive.

A Space Shuttle has three main parts: the orbiter, the fuel tank and rocket boosters.

At liftoff, the rocket boosters blast off with a force that carries the vehicle 27 miles high, at a speed of 3200 miles per hour, in just 126 seconds. At that point, the rockets separate from the orbiter and parachute back to Earth. The rockets are then picked up to be used again.

The orbiter is operated by astronauts as it orbits the Earth and completes its mission. Once the mission is accomplished, the orbiter re-enters the Earth's atmosphere and lands on Earth like a jet airplane.

Space Shuttles are used for different kinds of missions. They may carry scientists into space to conduct experiments. The Space Shuttle can service satellites already in orbit, or retrieve satellites to take back to Earth. The Space Shuttle's cargo bay contains a long robot arm that can move satellites in and out of the orbiter. The cargo bay will hold up to 32,000 pounds on its flight back to Earth.

Upon their return to Earth, Space Shuttles require about two weeks to prepare for a return flight into space.

A Space Shuttle is designed to carry 65,000 pounds of material, such as satellites or spacelabs, in the cargo bay on its trip into space. The materials, called payload, can be anything needed to be used or left in space.

• Tell why you would like to ride on a Space Shuttle.

Write.
The invention of the **Space Shuttle** has been a major advancement in space travel.

Page 45

The Space Shuttle   Name_____

Check.
Why was the one-time launching considered to be a problem?
- [✓] It was too expensive.
- [ ] It used one craft again and again.
- [✓] It required too much time to prepare new crafts.

Circle, check, write.
The Space Shuttle
. . .began to operate in the early (1980's) / 1970's
. . .is a launch vehicle which can
- [ ] be disposed of.
- [✓] be used again and again.
. . .greatly reduces the (cost) / weight of launching flights into space.
. . .will make it possible to build **spacelabs** in space.
. . .has three main parts:
the **orbiter**, the **fuel tank** and the **rocket boosters**.

Write 1, 2, 3, 4.
How does the Space Shuttle work?
(2) The rockets separate from the orbiter and parachute back to Earth where they are picked up to be used again.
(3) The orbiter is operated by astronauts as it orbits the Earth and completes its mission.
(1) At liftoff, the rocket boosters blast off and carry the vehicle miles into space.
(4) The orbiter re-enters the Earth's atmosphere and lands on Earth like a jet airplane.

Circle, write, check.
Space Shuttles are used. . .
to carry (scientists) / orbits into space to conduct **experiments**
to service **satellites** already in orbit.
to retrieve satellites
- [✓] to take back to Earth.
- [ ] to use as rockets.
The cargo bay. . .
- [✓] contains a long robot arm to move satellites in and out of the orbiter.
- [ ] contains teams of scientists.
- [✓] can hold up to 32,000 pounds on its flight back to Earth.

Page 46

Think About:
The Computer

One of the greatest inventions of the 20th century is the computer. A computer is a device that is used to store and process information and to perform calculations.

A computer can be designed to process almost any type of information. Computers are found in most businesses and industries. They are used in schools, hospitals and libraries. Computers are used by scientists and mathematicians, by doctors and lawyers, and by many other people in many kinds of work.

Computers can do practically anything—except think. Computers can only act on instructions which are entered into their systems; this set of instructions is called a program. A programmer enters instructions into the computer. These instructions are received in a storage unit called the memory. When information is needed, instructions and information are processed by the computer. This information is shown on a screen or printed on paper by a printer or an automatic typewriter.

The computer was not invented by just one person. As early as the 1600's, scientists and mathematicians developed devices for calculations. In the mid-1800's, several machines were developed to calculate numbers by following a set of instructions. But it wasn't until the 1930's and 1940's, that electronic computers were designed and built which could compute facts

the microchip

Name_____

in just seconds. The first modern computer was built in 1946; it was known as ENIAC. But this first electronic computer was huge—it required an entire room to hold it.

In 1947, the transistor was invented. With transistors, computers could be made much smaller and more powerful than ENIAC.

But the real breakthrough in computers came in the early 1970's, with the invention of the microchip. A microchip is about the size of a fingernail. The whole microchip unit is called a microprocessor. The microchip holds most of the important parts of a computer.

Because of the microchip, computers can be made much smaller and cheaper. The microchip makes it possible to produce the many microcomputers used today. The programs for microcomputers are called software. The microcomputer itself is called hardware.

Today, microcomputers are used to make everything from video games to space rockets.

• Make a list of things at home, school or in your neighborhood which are operated by microcomputers.

Page 47

The Computer   Name_____

Write.
A computer is a device that is used to **store** and **process** information and perform **calculations**.

True and False
Computers . . .
- T can be designed to process almost any type of information.
- F are special machines which are designed to think.
- T are found in most businesses and industries.
- F are built to work without further instructions.
- T are used by scientists, mathematicians, farmers and many others.
- T can only act on instructions which are placed into their systems.

Write 1, 2, 3, 4.
(2) The instructions are received in a storage unit called memory.
(3) When information is needed, it is processed by the computer.
(1) A programmer enters instructions into the computer.
(4) The information is shown on a screen, or printed on paper.

Underline.
As early as the 1600's. . .
scientists and mathematicians developed devices for calculation.
scientists designed programs for computers.
In the 1930's and 1940's. . .
electronic computers were small and easy to use.
electronic computers could compute facts in just seconds.

Circle, write, check.
The first modern computer was built in (1946) / 1935.
The computer was known as **ENIAC**.
ENIAC was [ ] tiny. [✓] huge. [ ] small enough to sit on a desk.
In 1947, the invention of the **transistor** made it possible for computers to be made smaller and more powerful than ENIAC.
In the early 1970's, the invention of the **microchip** provided the real breakthrough in computers.
A microchip is about the size of
[ ] a desk. [ ] a book. [✓] a fingernail. [ ] a T.V.
The whole microchip unit is called a **microprocessor**.

Answer Key

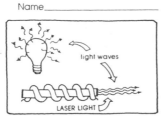

Think About:
The Laser

The invention of the laser has produced many advances in science. A laser is a special device for strengthening or amplifying light. The light from a laser is not the same as the light from electric bulbs, fluorescent lights or even the sun. Laser light is light that travels in a narrow beam in only one direction.

Because of the strength of laser light, it can be used in many areas, such as; medicine, industry, communications and scientific experiments.

Lasers are important in medicine. Surgeons use the heat of lasers to mend damaged tissue.

Lasers are important in industry. Workers use the intense heat from a laser to melt or cut hard materials. Laser beams are also used to weld metal parts together.

Lasers are important in communications. Laser beams are used to carry television and voice signals over long distances.

Lasers are important in scientific experiments. Lasers are used to make hot gases called plasmas. Plasmas are used to study how energy is made.

There are 3 basic kinds of lasers: solid, gas and liquid.

Solid lasers are used more often than the other kinds of lasers. Solid lasers may be made of glass, crystal or a semi-conductor. Solid lasers are used most often in scientific research.

Gas lasers are frequently used in communications. Liquid lasers are used to study atoms and molecules.

The laser was invented in the early 1960's. The invention was possible because of the invention, ten years earlier, of the maser. The maser strengthens or amplifies microwaves. Scientists immediately began working to amplify light waves. In 1960, an American physicist, Theodore H. Maiman, built the first laser.

Lasers are being continually improved. They are even used by astronauts for space experimentation. The astronauts on the Apollo II flight left a laser refractor on the moon. This mirrored device has been used to measure the distance between the Earth and moon.

The word "laser" comes from the term—Light Amplification by Stimulated Emission of Radiation.

• From what you have read, draw a picture of what a laser beam might look like.

Write.
A laser is a special device for **strengthening** and **amplifying** light.

Page 48

The Laser

Write, check.
The light from a laser ☐ is ☑ is not the same as the light from electric bulbs, fluorescent lights or even the sun.
Laser light travels in a **narrow** beam in only **one** direction.
Because of the strength of laser light, it can be used in areas, such as:
medicine, **industry**, **communications** and **scientific experiments**.

Circle, check, underline, write.

Lasers
In medicine, surgeons use the (heat)/brightness of lasers to:
☑ mend damaged tissue.
☐ warm the surgical instruments.
In industry, workers use the heat of lasers to:
☑ melt or cut hard material.
☐ light large storage areas.
☑ weld metal parts together.
In communications, laser beams are used . . .
to put more color into televisions.
to carry television and voice signals over long distances
In scientific experiments, lasers are used to make hot gases, called **plasmas**, which are used to study how water/(energy) is made.
The word intense means: ☐ hard, solid material.
☒ to an extremely high or strong degree.

Write.
The three basic kinds of lasers are:
solid, **gas** and **liquid**
    A   B   C

Write A, B, C.
__B__ Lasers frequently used in communications
__A__ Lasers used most often in scientific research
__C__ Lasers used to study atoms and molecules
__A__ May be made of glass, crystal or semi-conductor

Write.
The word laser comes from the term: L **ight** A **mplification** by S **timulated** E **mission** of R **adiation**

Page 49

Wonder About:

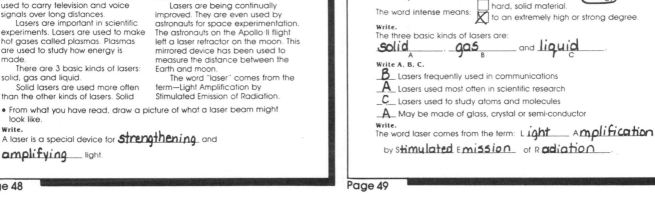

The Pyramids

The pyramids of Egypt are among the Seven Wonders of the Ancient World. Pyramids are huge, four-sided, triangular structures which rest on square bases. Pyramids were built in ancient times as tombs or temples for kings or rulers.

The first known Egyptian pyramid was built in 2650 B.C. for King Zoser. It was built by Imhotep, a famous architect, physician and statesman of Egypt. The tomb had an uneven texture and featured a series of giant steps on its sides. This pyramid, called the Step Pyramid, lies near Cairo, Egypt, on the site of the ancient city of Saqqarah.

The largest and most famous of all Egyptian pyramids are located on the west bank of the Nile River near Cairo. Known as the Three Pyramids at Giza, they are the best preserved of all pyramids. The largest of the three pyramids is called the Great Pyramid. It was built in 2600 B.C. as a tomb for King Khufu. The Great Pyramid consists of 2,300,000 blocks of stone, each weighing two and one-half tons. Standing over 450 feet high, its base covers over 13 acres—an area large enough to hold ten football fields.

Since the ancient Egyptians had no iron tools or machinery, they used copper chisels and saws to cut huge blocks of limestone. The blocks were dragged to the pyramids by gangs of workers. Ramps were built on which to drag the blocks of stone up the side of the structure to put in place. An outer layer of white casting stones gave the Great Pyramid a smooth, solid appearance.

Inside the Great Pyramid, corridors lead to several rooms, or chambers. The king's chamber was hewn out of solid stone. It is reached by a 153-foot passage called the Grand Gallery. A second, smaller chamber is called the Queen's Gallery, although the queen was buried in a separate, small pyramid. The third chamber was reached by a 320-foot corridor which descended deep below the ground level of the pyramid.

The other two of the three Pyramids of Egypt lie close by. One was built as a tomb for King Khafre. The other was built for King Mankaure. Near the pyramid of King Khafre stands the famous Sphinx at Giza, built in his honor.

Many of the priceless treasures and mummies buried in the pyramids were later stolen by thieves. Egyptian kings, fearful of this fate, were no longer buried in pyramids. They were buried in secret tombs in cliffs.

• From what you have read, draw a picture showing the chambers and corridors inside the Great Pyramid.

Page 50

The Pyramids

Underline.
The pyramids of Egypt are among the . . .
Seven Wonders of Ancient Egypt.
Seven Wonders of the Ancient World.

Check, circle, write.
The pyramids are huge, ☐ five-sided ☑ four-sided, (triangular)/octagonal structures which rest on **square** bases.

Pyramids were built as (tombs)/palaces or temples for kings.

The **1st** known **pyramid**
. . .was built in **2650** B.C. for King **Zoser**
. . .was built by **Imhotep**, a famous architect in Egypt.
. . .featured a series of giant carvings/(steps) on its sides.
. . .was called the **Step Pyramid**.
. . .lies near **Cairo**, Egypt, on the site of the ancient city of **Saqqarah**.

the Great Pyramid
. . .was built in **2600** B.C. as a tomb for **King Khufu**.
. . .consists of **2,300,000** blocks of stone.
. . .stands over ☑ 450 ☐ 1000 feet high.
. . .has a base which covers over **13** acres.

True or False
Inside the Great Pyramid . . .
True corridors lead to several rooms, or chambers.
False the King's Chamber was carved from gold.
True the King's Chamber is reached by a 153-foot passage.
False the queen was buried in the Queen's Gallery.
True a 320-foot corridor descends to a third chamber.

Write.
The other two pyramids of the Three Pyramids of Egypt were built as tombs for King **Khafre** and King **Mankaure**.
The famous **Sphinx** at Giza stands near the pyramid of King Khafre.

Page 51

Page 52

 **Wonder About:** Name_____

The Hanging Gardens of Babylon

The Hanging Gardens of Babylon are considered to be one of the Seven Wonders of the Ancient World. Built in the late 500's B.C., they were located in the city of Babylon, the capital of the ancient civilization of Babylonia.

The Hanging Gardens were built during the reign of King Nebuchadnezzar II. Historians believe that Nebuchadnezzar had the Hanging Gardens built for his wife Amyitis, who was homesick for her homeland, Media. While Media had been a land of cool, green hills, Babylon was surrounded by dry, flat land. To comfort his wife, Nebuchadnezzar designed a rooftop garden filled with trees and lush gardens.

Ancient historians described the gardens as "vaulted terraces, raised one above the other, resting on cube-shaped pillars". The pillars were hollowed out and filled with earth to allow large trees to be planted. The structure was built with baked brick and stones.

A Babylonian priest of the 200's B.C., named Berossus, described the gardens as rising 75 feet above the ground. The ascent to the top of the gardens was made by stairs. The lush gardens were laid out in terraces covering over 400 square feet.

To grow such trees, shrubs, plants and flowers required almost continuous watering, a difficult task in such hot, arid land. To accomplish this task, water was irrigated from the Euphrates River and lifted to the top of the gardens by a "pumping" system of buckets operated by workers. The watering process never stopped, which provided a constant flow of water through the gardens. The water was drained by layers of reeds and tiles to prevent the water from seeping into the rooms below the garden. Some water was probably allowed to trickle down the walls of the inner rooms to help keep them cool.

In 1899, a German archeologist named Robert Koldeway, began excavating a site believed to be the location of ancient Babylonia. Within weeks, he had located what he believed to be the ruins of the Hanging Gardens of Babylon. Underneath this area he discovered a cellar of fourteen rooms, one of which contained a kind of pumping station of wheels and buckets. Koldeway believed this was the remains of the system used to hoist water up to the gardens.

It is hard to imagine how incredible the gardens must have seemed in such dry land.

- Imagine that you live in ancient Babylon. Describe what you would see and think on a visit to the Hanging Gardens.

Page 52

Page 53

Hanging Gardens of Babylon   Name_____

Write, check.
The Hanging Gardens were built in the late **500** 's B.C.
in the city of ☐ Babylonia. ☑ Babylon.
Babylon was the capital of the ancient civilization **of Babylonia.**
The Hanging Gardens were built during the reign of
King **Nebuchadnezzar** II for his wife, **Amyitis** .
Amyitis was homesick for her homeland, ☐ Rhodes.
                                    ☑ Media.
Match, check.
  Media ╳ surrounded by dry, flat land
  Babylon ╳ a land of cool, green hills
To comfort his homesick wife, Nebuchadnezzar designed . . .
a ☑ rooftop   garden filled with: ☑ trees ☑ lush gardens
  ☐ covered   ☐ statues ☐ walks
Underline the sentences which tell how an ancient historian described the gardens.
A Babylonian priest of the 200's B.C., named **Berossus** , described the gardens as . . .
  rising **75** feet above the ground.
  reached by ascending ☐ ladders ☑ stairs to the top.
  laid out on terraces covering over **400** square feet.
To grow the trees, shrubs, plants and flowers, water was irrigated from the
  Euphrates River, and lifted to the gardens by a " **pumping** " system.
Check, write, circle, underline.
In 1800,
  ⟨1899⟩ a German archeologist located . . .
  what he believed to be the ruins of the Hanging Gardens,
  trees, plants, and shrubs from the Hanging Gardens.

Koldeway found a ☐ palace of ☐ 40   rooms which contained a kind of
               ☑ cellar   ☑ 14
pumping station of **wheels** and **buckets** .
Koldeway believed this system was used to ☐ lower ☑ hoist water to the gardens.

Page 53

Page 54

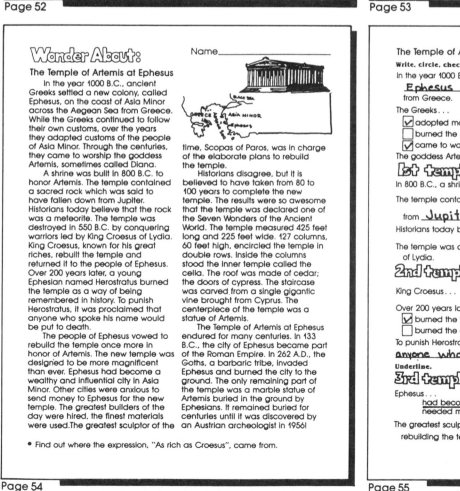 **Wonder About:** Name_____

The Temple of Artemis at Ephesus

In the year 1000 B.C., ancient Greeks settled a new colony, called Ephesus, on the coast of Asia Minor across the Aegean Sea from Greece. While the Greeks continued to follow their own customs, over the years they adapted customs of the people of Asia Minor. Through the centuries, they came to worship the goddess Artemis, sometimes called Diana.

A shrine was built in 800 B.C. to honor Artemis. The temple contained a sacred rock which was said to have fallen down from Jupiter. Historians today believe that the rock was a meteorite. The temple was destroyed in 550 B.C. by conquering warriors led by King Croesus of Lydia. King Croesus, known for his great riches, rebuilt the temple and returned it to the people of Ephesus. Over 200 years later, a young Ephesian named Herostratus burned the temple as a way of being remembered in history. To punish Herostratus, it was proclaimed that anyone who spoke his name would be put to death.

The people of Ephesus vowed to rebuild the temple once more in honor of Artemis. The new temple was designed to be more magnificent than ever. Ephesus had become a wealthy and influential city in Asia Minor. Other cities were anxious to send money to Ephesus for the new temple. The greatest builders of the day were hired, the finest materials were used. The greatest sculptor of the time, Scopas of Paros, was in charge of the elaborate plans to rebuild the temple.

Historians disagree, but it is believed to have taken from 80 to 100 years to complete the new temple. The results were so awesome that the temple was declared one of the Seven Wonders of the Ancient World. The temple measured 425 feet long and 225 feet wide. 127 columns, 60 feet high, encircled the temple in double rows. Inside the columns stood the inner temple called the cella. The roof was made of cedar; the doors of cypress. The staircase was carved from a single gigantic vine brought from Cyprus. The centerpiece of the temple was a statue of Artemis.

The Temple of Artemis at Ephesus endured for many centuries. In 133 B.C., the city of Ephesus became part of the Roman Empire. In 262 A.D., the Goths, a barbaric tribe, invaded Ephesus and burned the city to the ground. The only remaining part of the temple was a marble statue of Artemis buried in the ground by Ephesians. It remained buried for centuries until it was discovered by an Austrian archeologist in 1956!

- Find out where the expression, "As rich as Croesus", came from.

Page 54

Page 55

The Temple of Artemis at Ephesus   Name_____

Write, circle, check.
In the year 1000 B.C., ancient Greeks settled a new colony, called
  Ephesus , on the coast of Asia Minor across the **Aegean** Sea from Greece.
The Greeks . . .
  ☑ adopted many customs of the people of Asia Minor.
  ☐ burned the cities in Asia Minor.
  ☑ came to worship the goddess Artemis.
The goddess Artemis was also called ☐ Helena. ☑ Diana.
1st temple
In 800 B.C., a shrine was built to honor **Artemis** .
The temple contained a ⟨statue of Zeus⟩ which was said to have fallen
                        sacred rock
from **Jupiter** .
Historians today believe the rock was a **meteorite** .
The temple was destroyed in 650 B.C. by warriors led by King **Croesus**
                          ⟨550⟩
of Lydia.
2nd temple
King Croesus . . . ☐ built a monument to himself.
                  ☑ rebuilt the temple for the people of Ephesus.
Over 200 years later, a young Ephesian named **Herostratus**
  ☑ burned the temple as a way of being remembered.
  ☐ burned the city as a way of being remembered.
To punish Herostratus, it was proclaimed that:
anyone who spoke his name would be put to death.
Underline.
3rd temple – The Temple of Artemis
Ephesus . . .
  had become a wealthy and influential city in Asia Minor.
  needed money to be able to build a new temple.
The greatest sculptor of the time, **Scopas** of **Paros** , was in charge of rebuilding the temple.

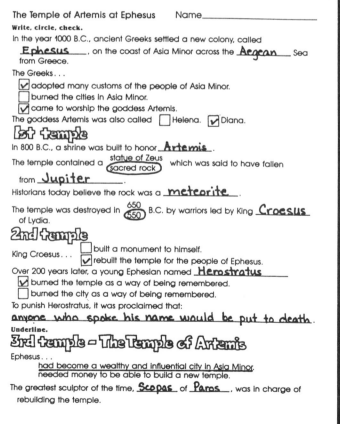

Page 55

Answer Key

Page 56

Wonder About:

Name_____

The Statue of Zeus at Olympia

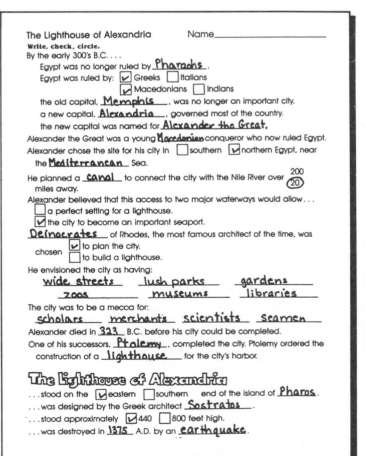

One of the most important places in ancient Greece was the holy shrine of Olympia. Olympia was located by Mount Olympus, the home of the chief god, Zeus. For years, no one lived at Olympia except priests and officials who cared for the first small temples. But after the first Olympic Games took place in 776 B.C. on the plains of Olympia, the temples grew in popularity and importance.

The holy shrine of Olympia became the force for bringing many Greeks together for the festival of the Olympic Games every four years. So important were the Olympic Games that the four year cycle of time between the Games was called an Olympiad. Events in Greek life were then spoken of as having occurred in the "fifth Olympiad" or the "twentieth Olympiad".

The holy shrine of Olympia had two main sections: the Stadion, or stadium, where the Olympic Games were held, and the Altis, or sacred grove, where the holy temples were built.

By the fifth century B.C., Olympia was so renowned as a holy place that grand new temples were erected. The most splendid of these was the Temple of Zeus, which contained a statue of Zeus considered to be one of the Seven Wonders of the Ancient World.

The Temple of Zeus was built between 470 and 456 B.C. by Libon, a master architect from nearby Ellis.

The Temple of Zeus towered on a high platform over the grove of the Altis. The temple had thirteen huge columns on each side and six on each end. The white marble of the temple was decorated with red and blue paintings and elaborate

carvings. But the showpiece of the temple rested inside. Dominating the inner hall of the temple was the enormous statue of Zeus, the most famous statue in the ancient world. The statue was made by the great Athenian sculptor, Phidias, in 435 B.C. Phidias had also sculpted the great statue of Athena, which stood in the Parthenon on the Acropolis in Athens.

The statue of Zeus was an awesome and majestic sight to all who beheld it. Rising 40 feet tall, it showed Zeus on his throne. The golden throne was set with ivory, ebony and precious stones. Zeus' robe was made of gold and his flesh was carved of ivory. <u>His uplifted right hand held a figurine of Nike, goddess of victory. In his left, he held a scepter made of precious metals.</u>

The temple stood for many years, but was later ordered destroyed by a Roman Emperor.

- How many years would have passed between the 21st and 58th Olympiads?

Page 56

Page 57

The Statue of Zeus at Olympia   Name_____

True or False

True The holy shrine of Olympia was one of the most important places in ancient Greece.

False Olympia was a temple in ancient Athens.

True Olympia was located by Mount Olympus.

True Mount Olympus was the home of the chief Greek god, Zeus.

True For years, only the priests and officials of the temples lived at Olympia.

True The first Olympic Games took place in 776 B.C. on the plains of Olympia.

False Because of the Olympic Games, no one any longer cared for the temples.

True Because of the Olympic Games, the temples grew in popularity and importance.

Check, write.

The Temple of Zeus

...was built between _470_ and _456_ B.C.

...was built by _Libon_, a master architect from Ellis.

...towered on a high platform

☐ on Mount Olympus. ☑ over the grove of the Altis.

...had _13_ columns on each side and _6_ on each end.

...was made of ☑ white · ☐ black marble decorated with _red_ and _blue_ paintings and elaborate carvings.

...featured an enormous statue of _Zeus_.

The Statue of Zeus

...was the most famous statue ☑ in the ancient world.

☐ of all time.

...was made by the great Athenian sculptor, _Phidias_, in 435 B.C.

...was ☐ 20 ☑ 40 feet tall.

...showed Zeus sitting on a golden throne set with _ivory_, _ebony_ and precious stones.

Underline the sentences which tell what Zeus held in his hands.

The temple was destroyed by a _Roman Emperor_.

Page 57

Page 58

Wonder About:

Name_____

The Lighthouse of Alexandria

By the early 300's B.C., Egypt was no longer ruled by Pharaohs as it was during the age of the pyramids. The country was now ruled by Greeks and Macedonians. The old capital, Memphis, was no longer an important city. Instead, a new capital city, Alexandria, governed most of the country. The new city was named for Alexander the Great, the young Macedonian conqueror who now ruled Egypt.

Alexander chose the site for his city in northern Egypt near the Mediterranean Sea. He planned a canal to connect the city with the Nile River, over twenty miles away. This access to two major waterways would allow Alexandria to become an important seaport.

Deinocrates of Rhodes, the most famous architect of the time, was chosen to plan the city. The city he envisioned would have wide streets lined with columns, lush parks and gardens, zoos, museums and libraries. The city was to be a mecca, or attraction, for scholars, merchants, scientists and seamen. It was to become a great trading port and marketplace.

Alexander the Great died in 323 B.C., long before the city could be completed. But one of his successors, Ptolemy, continued the plan for Alexandria. When Ptolemy moved to the completed city, he carried the body of Alexander to be laid to rest in the city which carried

his name.

In 290 B.C., Ptolemy ordered the construction of a lighthouse for the city's harbor. The Lighthouse of Alexandria, which stood on the eastern end of the island of Pharos, was designed by the Greek architect, Sostratos. It stood approximately 440 feet high. The Lighthouse was built of three sections. The bottom section, or base, was square. It was used as a military barracks and as a stable for three hundred horses.

The middle section was long and narrow and had eight sides. It featured a balcony where food was sold to travelers who were visiting the lighthouse.

The top section was circular. It contained a beacon chamber where a fire continually burned. The fire's light could be seen over a hundred miles away.

The Lighthouse of Alexandria became so famous that the name of the island, Pharos, became the word used to mean lighthouse.

The lighthouse stood for centuries until about 1375 A.D. when it fell during an earthquake.

- Find out where 3 other cities named Alexandria (also named for Alexander the Great) are located.

Page 58

Page 59

The Lighthouse of Alexandria   Name_____

Write, check, circle.

By the early 300's B.C....

Egypt was no longer ruled by _Pharaohs_.

Egypt was ruled by: ☑ Greeks ☐ Italians

☑ Macedonians ☐ Indians

the old capital, _Memphis_, was no longer an important city.

a new capital, _Alexandria_, governed most of the country.

the new capital was named for _Alexander the Great._

Alexander the Great was a young _Macedonian_ conqueror who now ruled Egypt.

Alexander chose the site for his city in ☐ southern ☑ northern Egypt, near the _Mediterranean_ Sea.

He planned a _canal_ to connect the city with the Nile River over ~~200~~ ⟨20⟩ miles away.

Alexander believed that this access to two major waterways would allow...

☐ a perfect setting for a lighthouse.

☑ the city to become an important seaport.

Deinocrates of Rhodes, the most famous architect of the time, was

chosen ☑ to plan the city.

☐ to build a lighthouse.

He envisioned the city as having:

wide streets   _lush parks_   _gardens_

zoos   _museums_   _libraries_

The city was to be a mecca for:

scholars   _merchants_   _scientists_   _seamen_

Alexander died in _323_ B.C. before his city could be completed.

One of his successors, _Ptolemy_, completed the city. Ptolemy ordered the construction of a _lighthouse_ for the city's harbor.

The Lighthouse of Alexandria

...stood on the ☑ eastern ☐ southern end of the island of _Pharos_.

...was designed by the Greek architect _Sostratos_.

...stood approximately ☑ 440 ☐ 800 feet high.

...was destroyed in _1375_ A.D. by an _earthquake_.

Page 59

Answer Key

Wonder About:
The Colossus of Rhodes

The Colossus of Rhodes was one of the Seven Wonders of the Ancient World. The word colossus comes from the Greek word colossos, which refers to any statue larger than life size. Although there were many famous larger-than-life statues in the ancient world, only one was given the name Colossus—that was the Colossus of Rhodes.

Rhodes is an island in the Aegean Sea near the southwestern tip of Asia Minor. Its location made it an important place for ships to stop as they sailed back and forth from the Mediterranean and the Aegean Seas. This connection with many parts of the world made Rhodes an extremely developed culture for its time.

In the early 400's B.C., Rhodes was under the control of Athens, Greece. In the 350's B.C., Rhodes was conquered by King Mausolus of Halicarnassus, a city on the coast of nearby Asia Minor. By 332 B.C., Rhodes had been captured by Alexander the Great. After Alexander's death in 323 B.C., his empire was divided into three parts, each governed by one of Alexander's three main generals—Ptolemy, Seleucus and Antigonus.

The island of Rhodes chose to be ruled by Ptolemy, who also ruled Egypt. This angered Antigonus, who decided to punish Rhodes for refusing to choose him as their leader. Antigonus sent his son Demetrius and

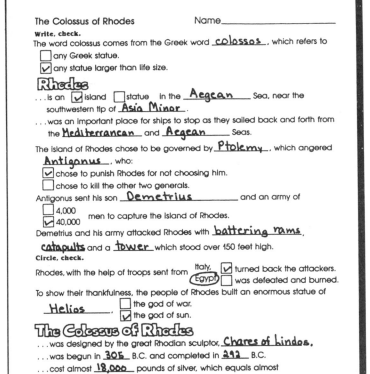

an army of 40,000 men to capture the island of Rhodes.

For months, Demetrius and his army attacked Rhodes. They used battering rams, catapults and a tower which stood over 150 feet high to try to break into the cities. But the Rhodians held fast, and later, with the help of troops sent by Ptolemy from Egypt, they turned back the attackers.

To show their thankfulness for being saved from their enemies, the people of Rhodes set out to build an enormous statue of Helios, the god of sun.

The great Rhodian sculptor, Chares of Lindos, was given the honor of designing and building the statue. Historians have recorded that the huge bronze statue was begun in 305 B.C. and completed in 292 B.C. It cost almost 18,000 pounds of silver, which would equal approximately five million dollars today. The statue stood almost 120 feet tall—about the same height as the Statue of Liberty.

In 224 B.C., only 68 years after completion, the Colossus of Rhodes was toppled by an earthquake. For centuries, the pieces of the statue lay where they fell. In 653 A.D., conquering Arabs sold the metal pieces of the great statue—for scrap.

• Name another harbor which has a famous statue at its entrance.

Page 60

The Colossus of Rhodes
Name_____

Write, check.

The word colossus comes from the Greek word __colossos__, which refers to
- [ ] any Greek statue.
- [✓] any statue larger than life size.

Rhodes

...is an [✓] island [ ] statue in the __Aegean__ Sea, near the southwestern tip of __Asia Minor__.

...was an important place for ships to stop as they sailed back and forth from the __Mediterranean__ and __Aegean__ Seas.

The island of Rhodes chose to be governed by __Ptolemy__, which angered __Antigonus__, who:
- [✓] chose to punish Rhodes for not choosing him.
- [ ] chose to kill the other two generals.

Antigonus sent his son __Demetrius__ and an army of
- [ ] 4,000
- [✓] 40,000
men to capture the island of Rhodes.

Demetrius and his army attacked Rhodes with __battering rams__, __catapults__ and a __tower__ which stood over 150 feet high.

Circle, check.

Rhodes, with the help of troops sent from Italy, (Egypt)
- [✓] turned back the attackers.
- [ ] was defeated and burned.

To show their thankfulness, the people of Rhodes built an enormous statue of __Helios__,
- [ ] the god of war.
- [✓] the god of sun.

The Colossus of Rhodes

...was designed by the great Rhodian sculptor, __Chares of Lindos.__

...was begun in __305__ B.C. and completed in __292__ B.C.

...cost almost __18,000__ pounds of silver, which equals almost
- [ ] one [✓] five million dollars.

...stood almost __120__ feet tall.

...was toppled by an
- [✓] earthquake,
- [ ] army,
__68__ years after it was built.

Page 61

Wonder About:

The Mausoleum at Halicarnassus

In 337 B.C., a Greek named Mausolus controlled most of southwestern Asia Minor, across the Aegean Sea from Greece. Many of the coastal cities of Asia Minor were inhabited by Greeks. Halicarnassus, the capital city of that region, was 60 miles south of Ephesus, where the great Temple of Artemis was located.

As the king, Mausolus worked hard to develop the city of Halicarnassus, where he lived in a splendid palace with his wife Artemisia. Queen Artemisia was named for the goddess Artemis.

When King Mausolus died in 353 B.C., Queen Artemisia vowed to build the world's most beautiful tomb in his honor.

Messengers carried the word through Greece that the most gifted artists and craftsmen were needed for the project. Scopas, who had guided the construction of the Temple of Artemis at Ephesus, came to Halicarnassus, as did the great architects, Satyros and Pythias. Thousands of other Greeks sailed across the Aegean to Halicarnassus to help build the tomb for Mausolus.

The monument was built high atop a hill overlooking the city. It was surrounded by a huge wall which enclosed a rectangular courtyard. In the center of the courtyard stood a stone platform which could be ascended by a flight of marble steps. The steps were flanked by sculptured lions. The tomb was built on this

platform, surrounded by thirty-six columns. A pyramidal structure was built above the tomb. It featured a marble statue of Mausolus in a chariot. The entire building stood over 140 feet high. The completed monument became one of the Seven Wonders of the Ancient World.

Queen Artemisia did not live to see the monument completed. She was buried by her husband in the tomb.

For centuries, the stunning monument stood undisturbed in Halicarnassus. Then, through a series of earthquakes and invasions, most of the structure was toppled. Today, only pieces of the once great building remain.

The tomb for Mausolus was so elaborate and famous that his name has been used to make a new word, mausoleum, which now describes any large tomb. Thus the name, The Mausoleum at Halicarnassus, has been given to one of the Seven Wonders of the Ancient World.

• Which of the other six Wonders of the Ancient World might be called a mausoleum?

Page 62

The Mausoleum of Halicarnassus
Name_____

Write, check, circle.

In 337 B.C., a Greek named __Mausolus__ controlled most of southwestern Asia Minor, across the __Aegean__ Sea from Greece.

Many of the coastal cities of Asia were inhabited by [ ] Italians. [✓] Greeks.

The capital city of that area was __Halicarnassus.__

Halicarnassus was 60 miles south of Athens (Ephesus.)

King Mausolus lived in Halicarnassus with his wife, Queen __Artemisia__, who was named for the goddess __Artemis__.

Underline, check, write, circle.

When King Mausolus died in [ ] 553 B.C. [✓] 353 B.C., Queen Artemisia vowed to become a great ruler. <u>Queen Artemisia vowed to build the world's most beautiful tomb in his honor.</u>

The Mausoleum at Halicarnassus

...was built atop a __hill__ overlooking the city.

...was surrounded by a moat (huge wall) which enclosed a courtyard.

...was reached by ascending a flight of...
- [✓] marble steps flanked by sculptures of lions.
- [ ] steps flanked by waterfalls.

...featured a marble statue of
- [✓] Mausolus in a chariot.
- [ ] the Greek god, Zeus.

...stood over __140__ feet high.

Queen Artemisia...
- [✓] did not live to see the monument completed.
- [ ] celebrated the completion of the monument with a festival.
- [✓] was buried by her husband in the tomb.

Today, the word mausoleum means:
- [✓] a large tomb.
- [ ] a king's monument.

Underline the sentence which tells how the Mausoleum at Halicarnassus was destroyed.

The Mausoleum at Halicarnassus was one of the __Seven Wonders of the Ancient World__.

Page 63

Answer Key

Page 64

Wonder About:

Acropolis

Name_____

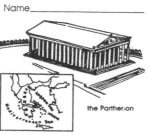

the Parthenon

The Acropolis, located in Athens, Greece, is the site of some of the most famous ruins from an ancient civilization. The word Acropolis means "upper city". It refers to the citadel, or highest part of a Greek city, around which the city was built. The hill served as a religious center, and sometimes even a fortress for the city.

The Acropolis in Athens, Greece, rises over 200 feet above the city. During the reign of Pericles, in the 400's B.C., the Parthenon was built on the Acropolis. The Parthenon, today considered the finest building of ancient Greece, was a temple built in honor of Athena, the patron goddess of Athens. The Parthenon, more than 100 feet wide and 230 feet long, is the world's finest example of Doric architecture. The temple was designed by Ictinus and Callicrates. The famous Greek sculptor, Phidias, directed its decoration. The Parthenon, made of white marble, featured a gold and ivory statue of Athena.

The Parthenon stood virtually unchanged for almost a thousand years. In the 500's A.D., it was used as a Christian church. In 1458, it was turned into a mosque by invading Turks. But in 1687, the Parthenon was hit by a shot from a Venetian ship. Gun powder, stored by the Turks in the cellars, exploded and caused great damage.

Today, some of the remaining artwork from the Parthenon is housed in museums. The ruins of the Parthenon still display elaborate carvings of legendary battles between men and centaurs and religious scenes honoring Athena.

Another temple built on the Acropolis, called the Erechtheum, held the oldest known image of Athena.

On the west side of the Acropolis stands the Temple of Athena Nike, which was completed in 424 B.C. Its famous frieze, or carved decorated band, depicts the Battle of Plataea, in which the Greeks defeated the Persians.

Today, these and many other buildings on the Acropolis are being preserved. But many of the statues, ornaments and frescoes no longer remain on the Acropolis. Some have been destroyed over the centuries; others have been taken by invading countries. A few have been removed and are kept in museums.

- Find out more about the goddess Athena and what she meant to the ancient Athenians.

Page 64

Page 65

The Acropolis ...

Name_____

True or False

The Acropolis...

True is located in Athens, Greece.
False is a famous seaport in Athens.
True means "upper city".
True is the highest part of the city.
False was used to store the city's food and water.
True served as a religious center in ancient Athens.
True sometimes served as a fortress for the city.
False rises over 1000 feet above the city of Athens.
True is the site of famous ruins from ancient Athens.

Check, write, underline.

The most famous building on the Acropolis is called the:
☐ Athena   ☐ Doric   ☑ Parthenon   ☐ Phidias

The Parthenon was built during the reign of **Pericles** In the ☐ 500's ☑ 400's B.C.

The Parthenon is considered to be...
the finest building of ancient Greece.
the first building of ancient Greece.

The Parthenon was a temple built in honor of **Athena**
☑ the patron goddess of Athens.   ☐ the goddess of war.

The Parthenon measures over **100** feet wide and **230** feet long.

...is the world's finest example of **Doric** architecture.
...was designed by **Ictinus** and **Callicrates**.
...was built under the direction of **Phidias**,
☐ the famous Greek ruler.
☑ the famous Greek sculptor.
...was made of ☑ white marble.   ☐ buff limestone.
...featured a **gold** and **ivory** statue of ☐ Zeus. ☑ Athena.

Underline the sentence which tells what battle is depicted on the frieze in the Temple of Athena Nike.

Page 65

Page 66

Wonder About:

Stonehenge

Name_____

On Salisbury Plain, 10 miles north of Wiltshire, England, stands the mysterious prehistoric monument called Stonehenge. The standing group of stones has been the object of speculation and study for centuries. Because of the specific arrangement of the stones, some scholars believe that Stonehenge may have been the site of sun worship or used as an astronomical temple for the study of days, seasons and years.

Archeologists are not sure why Stonehenge was built, but they believe they know how. The monument appears to be the result of three different construction periods. The first began approximately 1800 B.C. During this time, a circular bank about 327 feet across was built which featured an entrance on the northeast side. Located inside was a circle of 56 pits. They are named the Aubrey Holes for John Aubrey, who discovered them in the 1600's. Outside the entrance stands a 35-ton stone called the Heel Stone.

Almost a century later, the second period of construction began when the first standing stones were added to the monument. These famous blue stones are believed to have come from the Prescelly Mountains over 140 miles away! The stones were placed in two concentric circles (one within the other).

After another century had passed, blocks of sandstone, called sarsen, were brought from the Marlborough Downs over 20 miles away. These 50-ton blocks were used to form a circle of standing stones with horizontal stones lying on top of them. Scientists believe that the builders used stone hammers to produce their work, which included some amazing features. For instance, the top horizontal stones were curved to form the circle. Also, the stones had notches which allowed them to fit exactly on the standing stones. Inside the circle lies a single block, the Altar Stone.

In 1963, Gerald S. Hawkins, from the Smithsonian Observatory, made a study of Stonehenge. He concluded that there was a direct correlation between the placement of the stones and the rising and setting of the sun and moon in the year 1500 B.C. He concluded that Stonehenge may have been built as an astronomical calendar, which could be used to predict seasons of the year, and eclipses of the moon and sun.

Today, the British government is working to restore and protect Stonehenge.

- Imagine that you lived during the time Stonehenge was built. What would you have used Stonehenge for?

Page 66

Page 67

Stonehenge

Name_____

Write, check.

Stonehenge

...is located on **Salisbury Plain**, 10 miles north of **Wiltshire**, England.
...is believed to have been the site of ☑ sun worship. ☐ many battles.
...may have been used as an astronomical temple for the study of **days**, **seasons** and **years**.

Archeologists believe that Stonehenge is the result of ☐ eight ☑ three different construction periods.

1st construction period

The first construction period began in ☑ 1800 B.C. ☐ 1800 A.D.

A **circular** bank, measuring ☐ 300 ☑ 327 feet across, featured an entrance on the **northeast** side.

Located inside was a circle of **56** pits, named the **Aubrey Holes**.

Outside the entrance stands a **35**-ton stone called the **Heel Stone**.

2nd construction period

The second construction period began ☐ 1000 years later. ☑ a century later.

The first ☐ carved ☑ standing stones were added.

These famous ☐ limestones ☑ bluestones are believed to have come from the **Prescelly** Mountains over **140** miles away.

The stones are placed in **two concentric** circles.

3rd construction period

The third construction period began...
☑ after another century had passed.
☐ several thousands of years later.

These 50-ton blocks were used to form...
☐ a building surrounded by 48 columns.
☑ a circle of standing stones with horizontal stones lying on top of them.

Inside the circle lies a single block called the **Altar Stone**.

Page 67

Answer Key

Page 68

Wonder About:

The Great Wall of China

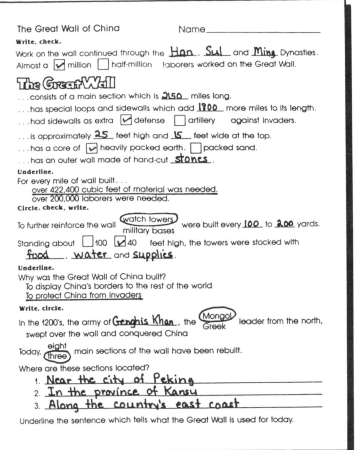

Name_____

The Great Wall of China, the longest structure ever built, is one of the most incredible man-made wonders in the world. Constructed entirely by hand, the Great Wall winds 4,000 miles across northern China.

During the 400's B.C., small stretches of the wall were built to protect the country from invaders. During the Ch'in Dynasty, from 221-206 B.C., these first walls were connected together in a new and much longer wall. Work on the wall continued through the Han, Sui and Ming dynasties. It has been estimated that almost a million laborers worked on the Great Wall over a period of many years.

The main part of the Great Wall stretches 2,150 miles long. Special sections of loops and sidewalls add 1,800 more miles to the length of the wall. These sidewalls were added as an extra defense against invaders. The wall is approximately 25 feet high, and 15 feet wide at the top. The core of the wall was made with heavily packed earth. The outer wall was finished with hand-cut stones. For every mile of wall built, over 422,400 cubic feet of material was needed.

To further reinforce the wall, watchtowers were built every 100 to 200 yards in the wall. The towers, which are about 40 feet high, were stocked with food, water and supplies for the defenders on guard at the wall.

Although the Great Wall was built to protect China from invaders, it was only successful with minor attacks. In the 1200's, the army of Genghis Khan, the Mongol leader from the north, swept across the wall and conquered most of China.

Over the centuries, much of the Great Wall deteriorated. Today, three main sections of the wall have been rebuilt. One section is near the city of Peking. Another is in the province of Kansu in north-central China. The third restored section is along the country's east coast. The Great Wall no longer exists for defense. Instead, it has become a tourist attraction for people from all around the world.

• Write a paragraph telling why you think the Great Wall was not successful in protecting China against invaders.

Write, circle.

The Great Wall winds 4000 miles across ~~southern~~ (northern) China.

Page 68

Page 69

The Great Wall of China   Name_____

Write, check.

Work on the wall continued through the Han, Sui and Ming Dynasties.
Almost a ☑ million ☐ half-million laborers worked on the Great Wall.

The Great Wall

...consists of a main section which is 2150 miles long.
...has special loops and sidewalls which add 1800 more miles to its length.
...had sidewalls as extra ☑ defense ☐ artillery against invaders.
...is approximately 25 feet high and 15 feet wide at the top.
...has a core of ☑ heavily packed earth. ☐ packed sand.
...has an outer wall made of hand-cut stones.

Underline.
For every mile of wall built...
    over 422,400 cubic feet of material was needed.
    over 200,000 laborers were needed.

Circle, check, write.
To further reinforce the wall (watch towers)/military bases were built every 100 to 200 yards.
Standing about ☐ 100 ☑ 40 feet high, the towers were stocked with
food, water and supplies.

Underline.
Why was the Great Wall of China built?
    To display China's borders to the rest of the world
    To protect China from invaders

Write, circle.
In the 1200's, the army of Genghis Khan, the (Mongol)/Greek leader from the north, swept over the wall and conquered China

Today, (eight)/three main sections of the wall have been rebuilt.
Where are these sections located?
    1. Near the city of Peking
    2. In the province of Kansu
    3. Along the country's east coast

Underline the sentence which tells what the Great Wall is used for today.

Page 69

Page 70

Wonder About:

Angkor Wat

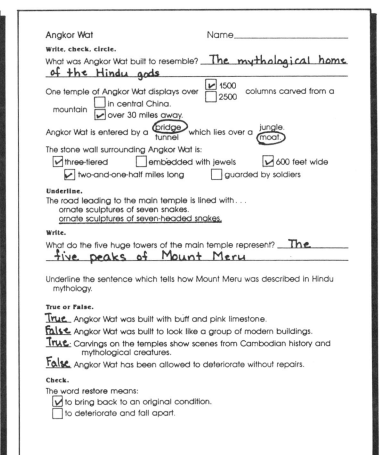

Name_____

One of the most incredible man-made wonders in the world is located deep in the jungles of Cambodia in Southeast Asia. The religious complex called Angkor Wat covers one square mile of land and contains temples and towers laid out in a pyramidal style.

Angkor Wat was built in the 1100's by the Cambodian King, Suryavarman II. He ordered the temple built in honor of the Hindu god, Vishnu. Suryavarman II was later buried in Angkor Wat.

Angkor Wat is considered to be the finest architectural monument in Cambodia. Its style was designed to resemble the mythological home of the Hindu gods. One temple alone displays over 1,500 columns, carved from a mountain over 30 miles away.

Angkor Wat can be entered by crossing a bridge that lies over a moat. The bridge leads to a three-tiered stone wall that stretches two-and-one-half miles long and 600 feet wide. Past this wall, lies a short road that leads into the main grounds of the temple. The road is lined with ornately carved sculptures of seven-headed snakes.

The main temple is crowned with five huge towers which represent the five peaks of Mount Meru. Mount Meru is described in Hindu mythology as standing 80,000 leagues high in the center of the earth.

Angkor Wat, built with buff and pink limestone, was created in such a way to look as if it were a large mountain of rock which had been carved with designs, instead of a building made of stones.

Many of the carvings on the temples of Angkor Wat depict scenes from early Cambodian history. Other carvings show mythical creatures, gods and goddesses.

Through the centuries, the humid air has caused damage to parts of Angkor Wat. But since the early 1900's, Cambodian and French archeologists have worked together to restore the buildings.

• From reading the story, draw a picture showing what the road leading to the temple might look like.

Underline.
Angkor Wat...
    is considered to be the oldest structure in Cambodia.
    is considered to be the finest architectural monument in Cambodia.

Page 70

Page 71

Angkor Wat   Name_____

Write, check, circle.

What was Angkor Wat built to resemble? The mythological home of the Hindu gods

One temple of Angkor Wat displays over ☑ 1500 ☐ 2500 columns carved from a mountain ☐ in central China. ☑ over 30 miles away.

Angkor Wat is entered by a (bridge)/tunnel which lies over a (moat)/jungle.

The stone wall surrounding Angkor Wat is:
☑ three-tiered   ☐ embedded with jewels   ☑ 600 feet wide
☑ two-and-one-half miles long   ☐ guarded by soldiers

Underline.
The road leading to the main temple is lined with...
    ornate sculptures of seven snakes.
    ornate sculptures of seven-headed snakes.

Write.
What do the five huge towers of the main temple represent? The five peaks of Mount Meru

Underline the sentence which tells how Mount Meru was described in Hindu mythology.

True or False.
True Angkor Wat was built with buff and pink limestone.
False Angkor Wat was built to look like a group of modern buildings.
True Carvings on the temples show scenes from Cambodian history and mythological creatures.
False Angkor Wat has been allowed to deteriorate without repairs.

Check.
The word restore means:
☑ to bring back to an original condition.
☐ to deteriorate and fall apart.

Page 71

Answer Key

Page 72

Wonder About:

Modern Wonder: Eiffel Tower

Name _____

The Eiffel Tower in Paris, France, is considered to be one of the Seven Wonders of the Modern World. The Eiffel Tower stands 984 feet high. It is made of a wrought-iron framework which rests on a base that is 330 feet square. The tower is made of 12,000 pieces of metal and 2½ million rivets. Elevators and stairways lead to the top of the tower. Among other things..the Eiffel Tower contains restaurants and weather stations. Since 1953, it has been used as the main television transmitter for Paris. Before that, it was used to transmit radio signals, and as a weather monitoring station.

Today, everyone agrees that the Eiffel Tower is a true wonder. But in 1887, many people believed that Alexander Gustave Eiffel was crazy when he began building his metal tower.

Gustave Eiffel designed his tower to be the centerpiece of the World's Fair Exposition of 1889 in Paris. He was chosen for the project because he was, at age fifty-three, France's master builder. Eiffel was already famous for his work with iron, which included the framework for the Statue of Liberty.

On January 26, 1887, workers began digging the foundation for the Eiffel Tower. Practically everyone but Gustave Eiffel believed that it would be impossible to finish what would be the tallest structure in the world in just two years. After all, it had taken 36 years to build the Washington Monument. Furthermore, the French government would only grant the project one-fifth of the money needed. Eiffel himself agreed to provide 1.3 million dollars which he could recover if the tower was a financial success.

In March of 1889, after over two years of continuous work, the Eiffel Tower was completed. Eiffel had not only met his deadline, but he had built the tower for less money than he had thought it would cost. The final cost was exactly $1,505,675.90.

When Gustave Eiffel died in 1923, the Eiffel Tower was still the tallest manmade structure in the world. Today, several buildings have surpassed the Eiffel Tower in height. But the Eiffel Tower, standing on the Champ de Mars in Paris, is still the tallest tower in the world!

• Write a story describing people watching the Eiffel Tower being built.

Write.

The Eiffel Tower

. . . is located in **Paris**, France

Page 73

Write.

The Eiffel Tower . . .
 stands **984** feet high.
 is made of a **wrought – iron** framework.
 rests on a base that is **330** feet square.
 is made of **12,000** pieces of metal.
 contains **2½ million** rivets.
 contains **elevators** and **stairways** that lead to the top.

Check, circle.
What has the Eiffel Tower been used for?
 ☑ television transmitter   ☑ weather monitor
 ☐ oil-drilling rig   ☑ radio transmitter

The Eiffel Tower contains (restaurants) bookstores and weather balloons. (weather stations.)

True or False

True The Eiffel Tower was designed for the World's Fair Exposition of 1899.
False Many people thought the Eiffel Tower could not be built.
False Gustave Eiffel was a well-known artist in Paris.
True Workers began digging the foundation on January 26, 1887.
False The Eiffel Tower took 3 years and 2 months to complete.
True At age fifty-three, Gustave Eiffel was France's masterbuilder.
False Gustave Eiffel had also designed the Washington Monument.

Check.
How much money did the French Government grant?
 ☐ 100 percent of the money needed
 ☐ 1.3 million dollars
 ☑ one-fifth of the money needed

Underline the sentence in the story which tells how much money Gustave Eiffel agreed to provide.

Write.
The final cost of the Eiffel Tower was $ **1,505,675.90**.

Write.
When Gustave Eiffel died in 1923, the Eiffel Tower was still . . .
the tallest manmade structure in the world.
Today, the Eiffel Tower is still . . .
the tallest tower in the world.

Page 74

Wonder About:

Taj Mahal

Name _____

The Taj Mahal is one of the most beautiful and elaborate man-made wonders in the world. It is located in the city of Agra in northern India.

Almost four centuries ago, in 1612, the Indian ruler, Shah Jahan, married an Indian princess. Shah Jahan called his wife Mumtaz-i-Mahal, which means, "pride of the palace". In 1631, Mumtaz-i-Mahal died. Her grieving husband decided to build an extravagant mausoleum, or tomb, for his wife and himself. He chose the banks of the Jumma River as the location for his monument.

It took more than 20,000 workers to build the Taj Mahal between the years of 1632 and 1653. The plans were drawn by a committee of architects from India, Persia and many parts of Asia.

The Taj Mahal is surrounded by walls which enclose rows of formal gardens and reflecting pools lined with cypress trees. These gardens lead to the mausoleum, which stands in the center of the grounds with two smaller buildings on either side.

The Taj Mahal, made of white marble, stands on an eight-sided platform made of red sandstone. Each side of the platform is 130 feet long. Each corner of the platform features a three-story, 138-foot-tall praying tower, called a minaret.

The mausoleum itself is almost 200 feet square. A great arch over 108 feet high is cut into each side of the building. The center part of the building is covered by a huge dome. The exterior of the building is decorated with passages from the Koran, the Moslem holy book.

Inside the Taj Mahal, elaborate decorations fill the walls. Precious stones, such as jasper, bloodstone, agates, cornelians and jade are inlaid in the marble walls to form pictures. In some cases, over 100 stones are used just to make one flower.

Marble walls of trelliswork, or carved designs, allow the sunlight to filter through the building in a soft glow. A center room contains two monuments called cenotaphs. A vault below the monuments holds the bodies of Shah Jahan and his wife.

• Find the names of three other famous tombs.

Write, check, circle.
The Taj Mahal is located in the city of **Agra**, in northern ☐ France. ☑ India.

Almost four centuries ago, in (1612) 1812, the Indian ruler, **Shah Jahan**, married an Indian princess.

Page 75

Taj Mahal

Name _____

Shah Johan called his wife **Mumtaz-i-Mahal**, which means "**pride**" of the "**palace**".

In 1631, Mumtaz-i-Mahal ☑ died. ☐ married.

The Taj Mahal was built as a ☑ mausoleum ☐ palace for Mumtaz-i-Mahal.

Shah Jahan chose the banks of the **Jumma** River as the location for the Taj Mahal.

It took more than **20,000** workers to build the Taj Mahal between the years of **1632** and **1653**.

The word mausoleum means: ☐ palace. ☑ tomb.

Underline.
The plans for the Taj Mahal were drawn by . . .
 a committee of architects from India, Persia and Asia.
 a committee of Indian rulers.

Write, check.

The Taj Mahal

. . .is made of ☐ carved jade. ☑ white marble.
. . .stands on an eight-sided platform made of **red sandstone**.
. . .features 138-foot-tall praying towers, called **minarets**.
. . .is almost ☐ 500 ☑ 200 feet square and is covered by a huge **dome**.
. . .is decorated with passages from the ☑ Koran. ☐ legends of India.

Check, write, circle.
The Koran is ☐ the ruler of India.
 ☑ the Moslem holy book.

The inside of the Taj Mahal is decorated with pictures made of precious stones, such as **jasper, bloodstone, agates, cornelians and jade**.

In some pictures, over **100** stones are used to make one flower.

A center room contains two monuments called vaults. (cenotaphs)

Underline the sentence which tells who is buried in the Taj Mahal.

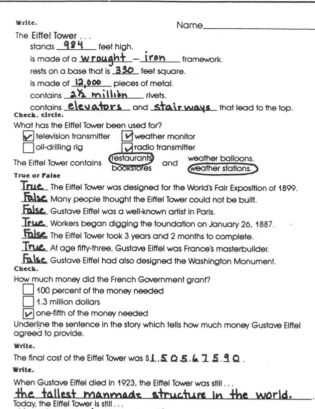

Page 76

Wonder About:
Suez Canal

Name_____

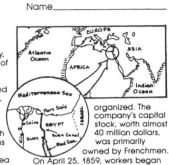

The development of the Suez Canal, a narrow, artificial waterway, was a modern man-made wonder of great significance. The waterway covers over 100 miles in Egypt to connect the Mediterranean Sea and the Red Sea. Because of the canal, which opened in 1869, the route between England and India was shortened by over 6,000 miles. The Suez Canal extends north and south through the Isthmus of Suez. It opens into the Mediterranean Sea at the city of Port Said and into the Red Sea at the city of Suez. Unlike many canals, the Suez Canal does not require locks, since the levels of the two seas are not significantly different.

When The Suez Canal was first built, it measured 230 feet wide and 26 feet deep. Since then, it has been enlarged to handle larger ships. Today, it measures 390 feet wide and 46 feet deep.

In 1799, Napoleon I first suggested a canal across the Isthmus of Suez after he visited Egypt. A French builder, Ferdinand de Lesseps, was put in charge of the plans. He received permission from Muhammad Said, the Viceroy of Egypt, to proceed with the project. The next year, an International Technical Commission met to decide on the exact route of the canal. A company to finance the project was organized. The company's capital stock, worth almost 40 million dollars, was primarily owned by Frenchmen.

On April 25, 1859, workers began construction of the Suez Canal. Ten years later, on November 17, 1869, the canal was officially opened.

Although Great Britain was a primary user of the Suez Canal, it did not buy shares of stock in the company until 1875. It then began sharing management responsibilities with France.

Although an international commission ruled that the canal would be open to all nations, during World Wars I and II, the canal was closed to enemies of Great Britain.

Until November 6, 1956, the United States, Great Britain, France, Israel and Egypt were not in agreement on how to control the canal. At that time, the United Nations stepped in and settled the dispute. In March of 1957, the canal was placed under the management of Egypt.

- Write a paragraph telling how different water travel would be without the Suez Canal.

Page 77

The Suez Canal   Name_____

Check, write, circle.

The Suez Canal
...is a narrow, artificial ☑ waterway. ☐ harbor.

...covers over **100** miles in **Egypt** to connect these two seas:
☑ Mediterranean ☐ Baltic ☐ Nile ☑ Red ☐ Arctic

...shortened the route between (England) and (China) by **6000** miles.
    Sweden   (India)

...extends **west** (north) and (south) **east** through the Isthmus of **Suez**

...opens into the Mediterranean Sea at the city of **Port Said**

...opens into the Red Sea at the city of **Suez**.

Underline the sentence which tells why the canal does not require locks.

Write 1-8.

How did the **Suez Canal** begin?

③ Muhammad Said gave permission for the project to proceed.
⑤ A company to finance the canal project was organized.
① In 1799, Napolean I proposed a canal after he visited Egypt.
⑧ On November 17, 1869, the canal was officially opened.
⑥ Company stock, worth 40 million dollars, was primarily owned by Frenchmen.
② A French builder, Ferdinand de Lesseps, was put in charge of the plans.
④ An International Technical Commission met to decide on the canal's route.
⑦ On April 25, 1859, workers began construction on the canal.

True or False

True In 1875, Great Britain began sharing management responsibilities with France.

False The canal was intended to be open to only five nations.

True During World Wars I and II, the canal was closed to enemies of Great Britain.

False On November 6, 1956, the United Nations settled a dispute between Israel and Italy.

True In March of 1957, the canal was placed under the management of Egypt.

Page 78

Wonder About:
Panama Canal

Name_____

When the Panama Canal was completed in 1914, it became one of the greatest engineering wonders in the world. Built by the United States, the canal is a waterway which cuts across the Isthmus of Panama to link the Atlantic Ocean and the Pacific Ocean.

Prior to the opening of the Panama Canal, ships traveling from one ocean to the other were forced to sail around South America. The canal meant that a ship sailing between New York and San Francisco would sail approximately 5000 miles, instead of the 13,000 miles required before the canal was opened.

For hundreds of years, people had known of the importance of a waterway across Central America. In 1903, the United States signed a treaty with Panama, which allowed the United States to build and operate a canal.

One of the first obstacles to overcome in building the canal was disease, which plagued the Isthmus of Panama. Special medical teams were sent to the area to improve sanitary conditions. Efforts were made to rid the area of mosquitoes which carried malaria and yellow fever.

In 1906, it was decided that the canal would be built by a series of locks, which would be cheaper and quicker to build. In 1907, an army engineer, Colonel George Goethals, was put in charge of the project. Construction began with three main tasks: to excavate tons of earth to clear passages, to build a dam across the Chagres River and create a new lake, and to build the series of locks.

Thousands of workers used steam shovels and dredges to cut passages through hills, swamps and jungles.

The completed canal was built at a cost of 380 million dollars. It runs 50 miles across the Isthmus of Panama from Limon Bay in the Atlantic to the Bay of Panama in the Pacific. The water in the canal is controlled by three sets of locks, or water-filled chambers. Each lock is 1,000 feet long, over 100 feet wide and 70 feet deep. All but the very largest of today's ships can pass through the canal.

In 1977, a new treaty was signed which made most of the canal zone part of Panama.

- Draw a map showing the route a ship would take from the Atlantic to the Pacific if there were no Panama Canal.

Page 79

Check, write, circle.   Name_____

The Panama Canal
...was completed in ☐ 1904. ☑ 1914.

...became one of the greatest (engineering) natural wonders in the world.

...was built by the ☐ country of Panama.
                   ☑ United States.

...cuts across the **Isthmus** of **Panama**.

...links the **Atlantic** Ocean and the **Pacific** Ocean.

Circle, write, check.

In **1803** **(1903)** the United States signed a treaty with **Panama**
    which allowed Panama to build and operate a canal.
    which allowed the United States to build and operate a canal.

One of the first obstacles to overcome in building the canal was **disease**, which plagued the Isthmus of Panama.

Special medical teams were sent:
☑ to improve sanitary conditions.
☐ to build ten new hospitals.

Efforts were made to rid the area of ☐ wasps, which carried
                                    ☑ mosquitoes,
malaria and **yellow fever**.

In 1906, it was decided that the canal would be built by a series of **locks**.

In 1907, Colonel **George Goethals** was put in charge of the project.

Construction began with three major tasks:
1. **To excavate tons of earth to clear passages**
2. **To build a dam across the Chagres River**
3. **To build the series of locks**

The word excavate means: ☐ to form a waterway.
                          ☑ to dig or scoop out earth.

The completed canal...
    was built at a cost of **380** million dollars.

runs ☐ 500   miles across the Isthmus of Panama, from **Limon Bay**
     ☑ 50
    in the Atlantic to the **Bay** of **Panama** in the Pacific.

Answer Key

Page 80

Wonder About:

The Brooklyn Bridge   Name_____

When the Brooklyn Bridge was opened on May 24, 1883, it was declared to be the "Eighth Wonder of the World". Spanning the East River in New York City, the Brooklyn Bridge joined the boroughs, or districts, of Brooklyn and Manhattan. At its opening, it was the longest suspension bridge on Earth. The bridge, with a span of 1595 feet, cost a total of 15 million dollars to build. The Brooklyn Bridge hangs, or is suspended, from huge steel cables approximately 16 inches thick. The cables are fastened to two gothic-style towers which stand 275 feet high at each end of the bridge. The bridge holds six lanes of traffic in addition to a unique walkway down its middle.

The building of the Brooklyn Bridge was one of the greatest architectural achievements ever. The credit belonged to a father and son, John A. Roebling and Colonel Washington A. Roebling. The Roeblings were pioneer builders of big suspension bridges. Prior to the Brooklyn Bridge, wrought iron had been used to support bridges. The Roebling's plan called for their new bridge to be built with steel-wire cables.

To hold the cables, the Roeblings had to first construct two large towers. These towers were built on huge foundations which were sunk in the riverbed and filled with concrete.

By 1877, the towers were completed, and work had begun on "spinning the cables". This process involved bunching steel wires together in compact bundles to form four, 16-inch cables. These cables were used to hold more than 1500 smaller cables which reached down to hold the bridge.

By the time the bridge opened in 1883, after 14 years of construction, twenty workers had died in accidents while building the bridge. John A. Roebling had also died as the result of an injury he had received while surveying the tower site. His son, Washington, managed to continue overseeing the project, but not without his own health problems. He developed the bends from working deep inside the bridge towers' bases. For months, he was confined to bed where he viewed the bridge (a quarter mile away) through his telescope. With the help of his wife, he still managed to supervise the completion of the bridge.

Today, the Brooklyn Bridge is still considered to be among the greatest engineering feats of all time.

• Find the names of three other famous suspension bridges.

Page 81

The Brooklyn Bridge   Name_____

Write, check.

When the Brooklyn Bridge was opened on May 24, _1883_, it was declared to be the "_Eighth Wonder_ of the _World_ ".

The Brooklyn Bridge spans the [✔] East [ ] Hudson River in _New York_ City.

The bridge joins the boroughs, or districts of _Brooklyn_ and _Manhattan_.

Underline.

At its opening, the Brooklyn Bridge...
    was the only suspension bridge on Earth.
    was the largest suspension bridge on Earth.

Write, check.

The bridge was built by a father, _John A. Roebling_, and his son, Colonel _Washington A. Roebling_.

The Roeblings...
    [✔] were pioneer builders of big suspension bridges.
    [ ] were also the builders of the Statue of Liberty.

Prior to the Brooklyn Bridge, _wrought iron_ had been used to support bridges.

The Roeblings plan called for the new bridge to be built with _steel wire_ cables.

The cables were held by [ ] steel beams.
                        [✔] two large towers.

Underline, write.

The cables were made by...
    bunching steel wires together in compact bundles.
    cutting sections of steel rods.

The cables were used to hold more than _1500_ smaller cables which reach down to hold the bridge.

Match.

John A. Roebling... ⟍   supervised the completion of the bridge.
Washington A. Roebling... ⟋   died before the bridge was completed.

Underline the sentence which tells how many workers died during the 14-year construction period.

Page 82

Wonder About:

Yellowstone National Park   Name_____

The Yellowstone National Park, located in the western United States, is the site of some of the most famous natural wonders in the world: geysers, hot springs, deep canyons, waterfalls and great evergreen forests. Yellowstone, the oldest national park in the United States, covers an area of land some 60 by 50 miles. Most of the land is located in the state of Wyoming, but it also spreads into Idaho and Montana. Scientists believe that the landscape of Yellowstone was created by a series of volcanic eruptions thousands of years ago. Molten rock, called magma, remains under the park. The heat from the magma produces the 200 geysers and thousands of hot springs for which Yellowstone is most famous.

Of all the wonders in Yellowstone, the main attraction is the famous geyser, Old Faithful. Approximately every 65 minutes, Old Faithful erupts for a period of three to five minutes. The geyser erupts in a burst of boiling water that jumps 100 feet in the air. Other geysers in the park produce a spectacular sight, but none are as popular as Old Faithful.

Geysers may differ in frequency of eruption and size, but they all work in much the same way. As water seeps into the ground, it collects around the hot magma. The heated water produces steam which rises and pushes up the cooler water above it. When the pressure becomes too great, the water erupts into the air. The cooled water falls back to the ground and the cycle begins again.

The magma under the park also produces bubbling hot springs and bubbling mud pools, called mudpots. The largest hot spring in Yellowstone, Grand Prismatic Spring, measures 370 feet.

Yellowstone Lake, which measures over 20 miles long and 14 miles wide, is the largest high altitude lake in North America. It lies almost 8,000 feet above sea level.

Ninety percent of Yellowstone Park is covered by evergreen forests of pine, fir and spruce trees. 200 species of birds are found in Yellowstone. More than 40 kinds of other animals live in Yellowstone, which is the largest wildlife preserve in the United States. Visitors to the park can see bears, bison, cougars, moose and mule deer.

The Yellowstone National Park offers more than 1,000 miles of hiking trails. More than two million persons visit the park each year.

• Write about safety tips for camping out in Yellowstone National Park.

Page 83

Yellowstone National Park   Name_____

Circle, check, write.

The Yellowstone National Park is the (oldest) / warmest park in the United States.

Yellowstone National Park covers an area of [ ] 5 square miles.
                                            [✔] 60 by 50 miles.

Most of Yellowstone National Park is located in the state of:
[ ] California   [ ] Idaho   [✔] Wyoming   [ ] Utah

The park also spreads into the states of _Idaho_ and _Montana_.

Name some of the famous natural wonders found at Yellowstone. _____
geysers, hot springs, deep canyons, waterfalls and great evergreen forests

Scientists believe that the landscape of Yellowstone was created:
    [ ] by water erosion for thousands of years.
    [✔] by a series of volcanic eruptions thousands of years ago.

Molten rock, called _magma_, lies under the park's soil.

The most popular attraction at Yellowstone is _Old Faithful_.

This attraction is a [ ] waterfall [✔] geyser which erupts every _65_ minutes for a period of _3_ to _5_ minutes.

Old Faithful's eruption sends boiling water
    [ ] across the park in winding streams.
    [✔] 100 feet in the air.

Write 1-5.

How is a **geyser** formed?
(2) The water, heated by the magma, produces steam.
(4) When the pressure becomes too great, the water erupts into the air.
(1) Water seeps into the ground and collects around the hot magma.
(5) The cooled water falls back to the ground.
(3) The steam rises and pushes the cooler water above it.

Check, write.

The magma also produces: [✔] hot springs [ ] canyons
                         [✔] mud pools [ ] gardens

The largest hot spring in Yellowstone is _Grand Prismatic Spring_, which measures [ ] 200 [✔] 370 feet.

Answer Key

Page 84

Wonder About:
Carlsbad Caverns

Carlsbad Caverns are among the most phenomenal natural wonders in the world. The underground system of caves and tunnels is believed to be the largest underground labyrinth in the world. Located about 20 miles southwest of Carlsbad, New Mexico, the Carlsbad Caverns extend for at least 23 miles.

Scientists believe that the caverns were formed as water penetrated and dissolved the underground limestone. The caverns extend at least 1,100 feet below ground. They display thousands of beautiful stalactites, hanging from the ceiling, and stalagmites, rising from the floor. These formations are made of aragonite and calcite, crystalline limestone which have built up over the years. The caverns receive their shades of red, yellow and tan from small amounts of iron ore and other minerals.

The largest area in the caverns is called the Big Room. It measures 1,300 feet long, 650 feet wide, and 300 feet high. The Big Room features rock formation called Rock of Ages and a 60-foot tall stalagmite called the Giant Dome. Other chambers are named King's Palace, Queen's Chamber, Green Lake Room and Papoose's Chamber.

For centuries, the entrance to the caverns, Bat Cave, was known to the Indians of that area. In 1901, a miner named James L. White discovered the caves. Because of his further explorations and enthusiasm, the

caverns became known to the rest of the country. On October 25, 1923, the Carlsbad Caverns were made a national monument. Later, the National Geographic Society organized a series of scientific explorations of the caverns. On May 14, 1930, the area was declared to be Carlsbad Caverns National Park. Originally, the park covered 700 acres. Today, it covers 73 square miles.

Visitors to Carlsbad Caverns are given a guided tour which begins at the natural entrance and covers a three mile route. Visitors can ride an elevator from the entrance directly to the underground lunchroom, located near the Big Room.

One of the most incredible sights for visitors to see occurs outside the caverns. Each night during the summer months, millions of bats fly out of the Bat Cave entrance. During the daytime, they hang in the cave on the walls and ceilings. But at night, they leave the cave to find food. It is believed that each night the bats consume 11½ tons of insects!

- Imagine that you have discovered a cave. List five safety tips for exploring this new-found cave.

Page 84

Page 85

Carlsbad Caverns

Write and underline.

Carlsbad Caverns are a system of __caves__ and __tunnels__ . . . which form the largest underground labyrinth in the world. which were formed within the last five hundred years.

Check.

The word labyrinth means:
- [✓] a system of passages much like a maze.
- [ ] an enormous, undergound cave.

Write, check.

Carlsbad Caverns

. . .are located __20__ miles southwest of Carlsbad, New Mexico.

. . .extend underground for at least __23__ miles.

. . .are believed to have formed . . .
- [ ] as the air decayed the rock and caused it to fall away.
- [✓] as water penetrated and dissolved the underground limestone.

. . .receive their colors of __red__ , __yellow__ and __tan__ from small amounts of [✓] iron ore [ ] gold and other minerals.

The caverns display beautiful formations called __stalactites__ , which hang from the ceiling, and __stalagmites__ , which rise from the floor.

These formations are made of crystalline limestone named __aragonite__ and __calcite__ .

The largest area in the caverns is called the -
- [ ] Bat Cave.
- [✓] Big Room.

The area measures: __1300__ feet long
__650__ feet wide
__300__ feet high

Check, write.

On October 25, 1923, Carlsbad Caverns became a:
- [ ] scientific reserve.
- [✓] national monument.

On May 14, 1930, the area was named __Carlsbad Caverns National Park__

Underline the paragraph which tells of the incredible sight seen each summer night at the entrance to the caverns.

Page 85

Page 86

Wonder About:
Mount Rushmore National Memorial

One of the most famous and recognizable manmade wonders of the world is found on Mount Rushmore in the Black Hills of South Dakota. Mount Rushmore National Memorial is a huge carving on a granite cliff which shows the faces of four of America's greatest presidents: George Washington, Thomas Jefferson, Theodore Roosevelt and Abraham Lincoln.

Mount Rushmore is located 25 miles from Rapid City, South Dakota. The cliff rises over 500 feet above the valley, and is 5,725 feet above sea level.

On August 10, 1927, thousands of people gathered at the base of Mount Rushmore to witness the first drilling on the mountainside by the man chosen to design and supervise the memorial, Gutzon Borglum. Borglum was a well-known sculptor, famous for his excellent technique and creativity. His previous works included the statue of Lincoln's head, located in the Capitol in Washington, D.C., and another statue of Lincoln seated on a bench, located in Newark, New Jersey. His statue, Mares of Diomedes, is displayed in the Metropolitan Museum of Art in New York.

Borglum began work on the monument by dividing the carving into a series of steps. The first step, called pointing, was an exact

drawing of each president's head which showed the precise place for putting each drill in the rock and the exact depth to which each drill could go.

The workers used "swing seats", invented by Borglum, to hang over the side of the cliff. From these seats, they were able to drill at each exact point. After drilling, the holes were filled with a certain amount of dynamite, which was detonated each day when all of the workers were off the mountain. By the completion of the memorial, over 450,000 tons of granite had been blasted away.

The first president to be finished was George Washington. His carved head was over 60 feet tall—as high as a five-story building. The work continued another eleven years until all four presidents were completed.

Borglum did not live to see the entire monument completed. After his death in 1941, his son, Lincoln, finished the famous project which his father had begun.

The unique memorial took 14 years and one million dollars to complete. Today, it stands as a national symbol which scientists predict can last for some five million years to come.

- If you were designing a new Mount Rushmore, which four presidents would you choose, and why?

Page 86

Page 87

Mount Rushmore National Memorial

Write, check.

Mount Rushmore National Memorial is located in the __Black__ Hills of __South Dakota__ .

It is a huge carving on a [✓] granite [ ] grassy cliff which shows the faces of __4__ American presidents. The presidents are: __George Washington, Thomas Jefferson, Theodore Roosevelt, Abraham Lincoln__

Write, check.

The man chosen to design and supervise the memorial was __Gutzon Borglum__
- [✓] a well-known sculptor.
- [ ] a well-known mountaineer.

Some of Borglum's previous works were:
1. __Statue of Lincoln's head in the Capitol in Wash. D.C.__
2. __Statue of Lincoln in Newark, New Jersey__
3. __Statue, Mares of Diomedes, in Metropolitan Museum of Art__

Yes or No

Pointing . . .
__Yes__ was an exact drawing of each president's head.
__No__ was a seat designed to hang over the cliff.
__Yes__ showed the precise place for putting each drill in the rock.
__Yes__ showed the exact depth each drill should go.

The workers used "__swing__ seats"
- [ ] store the dynamite.
- [✓] to hang over the side of the cliff.

Write 1, 2, 3, 4.

- ② Sitting in swing seats, the workers drilled at each exact point.
- ④ When the workers were off the mountain, the dynamite was detonated.
- ① The workers used pointing to mark the exact site for drilling.
- ③ The holes were filled with a certain amount of dynamite.

Check, write, circle.

The word detonate means:
- [✓] to cause to explode.
- [ ] to drill.

By the completion of the memorial, over __450,000__ tons of granite had been blasted away.

Borglum (did) (did not) live to see the memorial completed.

His son, __Lincoln__ , finished the project.

Page 87

Answer Key

Page 88

Wonder About:
The Sequoia

One natural wonder of the world is among the oldest and largest of living things on Earth. It is the sequoia, a tree that once grew in plentiful varieties in forests over much of the world. Today, sequoias are found mainly in California, where only two kinds of true sequoias—the redwood and the giant sequoia—still grow.

The redwood, which is the tallest living tree, is found in the coastal mountains of northern California and southern Oregon. Growing in this warm, moist climate, the redwoods reach over 300 feet high—as tall as a 30-story building. The trunks of redwood trees are often more than 10 feet in diameter, with the bark as thick as 12 inches. The redwood gets its name from the color of its wood, which turns from light to dark red as it weathers. Redwoods are sometimes called "California redwoods" or "coasts", since they grow along the Pacific coast of California.

The other true sequoia is the giant sequoia, which grows only on the western slopes of the Sierra Nevada Mountains of California. Once, the giant sequoias grew in many parts of the Northern Hemisphere. Today, they are found in only 70 groves high in the mountains at elevations of 5000 to 7800 feet. Although giant sequoias do not grow as tall as redwoods, their trunks are much larger. Some trunks are as large as 100 feet around the base.

The largest tree in the world is found in Sequoia National Park.

Name_____

Named the General Sherman Tree, it stands 272.4 feet high and measures 101.6 feet around its base. Scientists believe that this single tree could produce over 600,000 board feet of lumber!

The giant sequoia is classified as an evergreen tree. It grows scalelike needles up to ½ inch long and produces woody, oval-shaped cones about 2 to 3 inches long. Although lightning has destroyed the tops of many of the trees, they are considered to be among the hardiest of living things.

Scientists have dated many giant sequoias to be several thousand years old. The age is determined by counting the growth rings on a tree's trunk. Each growth ring stands for one year. Scientists have estimated that the General Sherman Tree is at least 3500 years old, and so it becomes not only the world's largest tree, but also one of the oldest living things on Earth.

• List ten events which have occurred during the life of the Sherman Tree.

Page 89

The Sequoia
Name_____

Write, check.

The Sequoia is among the __oldest__ and __largest__ of living things on Earth.

The Sequoia once grew
☐ only in extremely cold climates.
☑ in forests over much of the world.

Today, Sequoias are found mainly in __California__, where only
☑ two ☐ five kinds still grow:
__the redwood__ and __the giant sequoia__.

The Redwood
. . . is the ☑ tallest ☐ widest living tree.
. . . is found in the coastal mountains of northern __California__ and southern __Oregon__.
. . . grows to a height of __300__ feet.
. . . often have trunks more than ☑ 10 ☐ 20 feet in diameter with the __bark__ as thick as 12 inches.
. . . gets its name from:
☐ the color of the leaves as they turn in the fall.
☑ the color of the wood, which turns from light to dark red as it weathers.
. . . are sometimes called "__California redwoods__" or "__coasts__".

The Giant Sequoia
. . . grows only on the western slopes of the __Sierra Nevada__ Mountains of ☑ California. ☐ Oregon.
. . . once grew in many parts of the __Northern__ Hemisphere.
. . . is found today in only ☑ 70 ☐ 7 groves high in the mountains at elevations of __5000__ to __7800__ feet.

The largest tree in the world
. . . is found in the __Sequoia National__ Park.
. . . is named __the General Sherman__ Tree.
. . . stands __272.4__ feet high, and measures __101.6__ feet around the base.
. . . is estimated to be ☑ at least 3500 years old.
☐ a million years old.

Page 90

Wonder About:
Niagara Falls

Niagara Falls is one of the most spectacular natural wonders of the world. The famous Falls are supplied by the Niagara River, which connects Lake Ontario and Lake Erie. The Niagara Falls, located midway in the river, pour 500,000 tons of water a minute into a deep gorge. The water drops in two sections divided by Goat Island. The right-hand section forms the American Falls, which is 193 feet high and over 1,000 feet wide. The left-hand section forms the Horseshoe Falls, which is 186 feet high and 2,100 feet wide.

Scientists believe that Niagara Falls was formed after the last ice sheet from the Ice Age had withdrawn from the area. The surface of the land had been changed by the ice. This caused waterways and streams to develop new paths. The result was an overflow of Lake Erie which produced Niagara Falls. Scientists believe the Falls are approximately 20,000 years old.

The Falls are formed over an outer layer of hard dolomitic limestone. This covers a softer layer of shale. The shale is more easily worn away which causes the harder limestone to form an over-hanging edge. This allows the Falls to drop straight down at a sharp angle, which produces a spectacular sight. But through the years, the outer layer has broken off at times. This is causing the Falls to gradually move

Name_____

back up the river. This erosion is happening to the American Falls at the rate of 3 to 7 inches a year. But the edge of the Horseshoe Falls is being worn back at the rate of approximately three feet a year.

Through the years, Niagara Falls has been a tremendous attraction for sightseers. Observation towers and a special area, Cave of the Winds, behind the Falls, have allowed remarkable views. At night, the Falls are flooded with lights. A steamer, called the Maid of the Mist, takes visitors for a ride around the base of the Falls.

Niagara Falls has also irresistibly drawn daredevils who have wanted to test their courage. One such man, Charles Blondin, crossed the Falls on a tightrope in 1859. Four days later, he crossed again, only this time with a blindfold. A month later, he crossed for the third time carrying a man on his shoulders. And as if that weren't daring enough, he returned to cross the Falls once again—on stilts!

• Find out how Niagara Falls compares to Victoria Falls.

Page 91

Write, circle, check.
Name_____

Niagara Falls is located midway in the __Niagara__ River, which connects Lake (Ontario) Placid and Lake ☑ Erie. ☐ Washington.

Check.
Scientists believe Niagara Falls was formed:
☐ as a result of a volcanic eruption.
☑ after the last ice sheet from the Ice Age had withdrawn.

The surface of the land had been changed by the
☐ sun.
☑ ice.
☐ falls.

Waterways and streams developed
☐ less water.
☑ new paths.

Write, check.
This caused an overflow of Lake __Erie__, which produced Niagara Falls.
Scientists believe Niagara Falls to be approximately __20,000__ years old.
Niagara Falls flows over an outer layer of hard __dolomitic limestone__ which covers a soft layer of
☐ mud.
☑ shale.

The constant flow of water over the land is gradually. . .
☑ eroding the land. ☐ causing a shortage of water.

The word erosion means:
☐ soil becomes rich with minerals from the water.
☑ the surface of the earth is worn away by the action of the water.

The land under the __American__ Falls is eroding at a rate of 3 to 7 inches a year.
The land under the __Horseshoe__ Falls is eroding at a rate of approximately three feet a year.

True or False
__True__ Niagara Falls is a tremendous attraction for sightseers.
__False__ Visitors can only view the Falls from the bottom.
__True__ At night, the Falls are flooded with lights.
__False__ A plane called, The Maid of the Mist, flies visitors over the Falls.
__True__ Visitors can view the Falls from "The Cave of the Winds".
__True__ A daredevil crossed the Falls on a tightrope.

Answer Key

Page 100

Wonder About:

Easter Island

Name_____

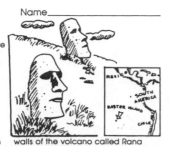

Few places in the world are more intriguing and mystifying than Easter Island, located in the Pacific Ocean 2,300 miles from the coast of Chile. Easter Island covers 63 square miles made up of rugged coastline and steep hills. Scientists believe the island began as a volcano. Three extinct volcanoes remain on the island, with the largest rising 1400 feet high.

On Easter Sunday of 1722, Dutch Admiral Jacob Roggevan and his crew landed on Easter Island aboard the Dutch ship Arena. The astonished crew found dozens of huge stone figures standing on long stone platforms. The statues, some measuring 40 feet tall, were similar in appearance. Their expressionless faces were without eyes. Huge red stone cylinders were placed on their heads. Since that time, the island has been a source of mystery and intrigue to scientists.

Archeologists believe that three different cultures lived on Easter Island. Around 400 A.D., the island was inhabited by a group of people who specialized in making small stone statues. Years later, another civilization tore down these statues and used them to build long temple platforms called ahus. These people carved more than 600 enormous stone busts of human forms and placed them on the ahus. Scientists believe that the statues were carved from hard volcanic rock in the crater

walls of the volcano called Rana Roraka. The statues were chiseled with stone picks made of basalt. <u>Although the statues weigh many tons each, it is believed that they were moved with ropes and rollers across the island and placed on the ahus.</u> Some ahus still hold up to 15 statues!

About 1670, another group of people invaded the island. These invaders practiced cannibalism. During this time, many people began living in underground caves where they hid their treasures.

In 1862, almost the entire population of Easter Island was wiped out by a smallpox epidemic carried to the island by Peruvian slave hunters.

In 1868, missionaries came to Easter Island and introduced the inhabitants to Christianity.

Today, Easter Island is governed by Chile, a country of South America. Almost the entire population of 1600 people live in the small village of Hanga Roa on the west coast of the island.

• Write your own ideas about what the Easter Island statues stand for, and why they were built.

Page 101

Write, circle and check.

Easter Island

Name_____

...is located in the <u>Pacific</u> Ocean, (2300) ~~1500~~ miles from the coast of <u>Chile</u>.

...covers <u>63</u> square miles made up of:
- ☑ rugged coastline ☐ meadows ☑ steep hills ☐ waterfalls

...is believed to have begun as a <u>volcano</u>.

...contains ☐ twenty-three ☑ three extinct volcanoes, with the largest rising <u>1400</u> feet high.

The term "extinct volcano" means: ☑ inactive. ☐ extremely hot.

On <u>Easter</u> Sunday of 17 <u>22</u>, Dutch Admiral <u>Jacob Roggevan</u> landed on Easter Island aboard the Dutch ship <u>Arena</u>.

Admiral Roggevan and his crew found:
- ☐ dozens of extinct animals.
- ☑ dozens of huge stone figures.

Write, underline.

Archeologists believe that <u>3</u> different cultures lived on Easter Island.

Around 400 A.D., Easter Island was inhabited by...
- a group of people who worshipped the sun.
- <u>a group of people who specialized in making small stone statues.</u>

Years later, Easter Island was inhabited by...
- <u>a group of people who tore down the original statues.</u>
- a group of people who painted the original statues.

Write, check.

These inhabitants
built long temple platforms called <u>ahus</u>.

They carved more than <u>600</u> stone busts of ☑ humans ☐ animals
from volcanic rock found in the volcano <u>Rana Roraka</u>.

Underline the sentence which tells how the statues were moved across the island.

Match.

1862 ⨉ Missionaries came to Easter Island.
1868   A smallpox epidemic killed many islanders.

Answer Key

Page 96

Wonder About:

The Sahara

Name_____

Stretching almost 3,000 miles across North Africa, the Sahara Desert is an incredible natural wonder of sand, rock and gravel. The Sahara covers over 3½ million square miles, which makes it by far the largest desert on Earth. It extends west to east from the Atlantic Ocean to the Red Sea.

The name Sahara comes from an Arabic word Sahra, which means desert. Because of the unusually low rainfall, even for a desert, the sun-scorched land and blistering winds make the Sahara the hottest region in the world during the summer. A sandy surface may reach a temperature of 170°F. The cloudless skies allow the daytime air temperature to reach 100°F. At night, the temperature often drops 40 to 50 degrees.

The Sahara's only vegetation is found near wells, springs or streams. These fertile areas are called oases. Some vegetation grows where the water table is close enough to the surface of the land to feed the roots of the plants. Throughout the desert are many dry stream beds, called wadis. During a rare rain, they will temporarily fill up with water.

The Sahara supports some animal life, too, such as camels, lizards and the addax, a desert antelope which carries a reserve of water in a sac within its body.

Some people of the Sahara live in tents which allows them to more easily move in search of grassy areas. These people, called Nomads, tend flocks of sheep, camels or goats. Others raise crops on land which has been irrigated.

Scientists believe that throughout the Ice Age, the Sahara was a rich grassland and hunting ground. Archeologists have recovered prehistoric relics which include stone tools and carvings of elephants, lions and giraffes. They believe that the Berbers, who live in northern Africa today, may be the descendents of the prehistoric people who once lived in that area. The Berbers are a tall, slender group of people with light skin and dark eyes and hair. They speak a language that resembles that of ancient Egypt. By the early ancient times, the Sahara was much as it is today.

Through the years, many plans to make the Sahara into fertile land again have not been successful. Some of these plans included digging artesian wells, or flooding areas with sea water from which the salt had been removed.

Today, the Sahara is being viewed as much more than a dry, hot desert. The discovery of rich oil and gas deposits underground have led to a modernization of transportation and the addition of pipelines to carry the oil hundreds of miles to the Mediterranean coast.

• Find out more about the Berbers and write a paragraph about them.

Page 97

Write, circle. Name_____

The Sahara

...is the **largest** desert on Earth.

...covers north to (east) from the **Atlantic** Ocean to the (west) south **Red** Sea.

Underline.

In the summer, the Sahara...
<u>is the hottest region in the world.</u>
receives no rainfall.

Match, write, check.

40° to 50°F ——— the temperature of the sand's surface
100°F ——— the number of degrees the temperature can drop at night
170°F ——— the daytime temperature

The Sahara's only vegetation is found near **wells** , **springs** or **streams** .

These fertile areas are called ☐ wadis. ☑ oases.

The desert contains dry stream beds called **wadis** .

The desert supports some animal life such as:
camels , **lizards** and **addax** .

Match.

Nomads ——— Tent dwellers who roam the desert in search of grassy areas
Berbers ——— May be descendents of prehistoric dwellers of the area

True or False

False. Scientists believe the Sahara was once covered with ice.

True. Scientists believe the Sahara was once a rich grassland.

True. Prehistoric relics have been recovered in the Sahara.

False. Berbers speak a language much like the ancient Greeks.

Write.

What new discovery has been made in the Sahara in recent years? **Rich oil and gas deposits**

How has this discovery affected the Sahara? **This discovery has led to a modernization of transportation and the addition of hundreds of miles of pipelines.**

Page 98

Wonder About:

Name_____

The Amazon River

The Amazon River is called the greatest river system in the world. This natural wonder is 4,000 miles long and contains more water than the Mississippi, the Nile and the Yangtze rivers together. Although the Nile River is 200 miles longer, the Amazon River is more massive. It drains over 2,500,000 square miles of land before it empties into the Atlantic Ocean at a rate of three billion gallons of water a minute. The Amazon River is over 200 miles wide at its mouth.

The Amazon River begins as the Apurimac River high in the Andes Mountains of Peru in South America. As the small river flows, it is joined by waters from other rivers. The river continues to flow eastward through Brazil until it empties into the Atlantic Ocean.

Much of the Amazon River covers an area that makes up the world's largest tropical rain forest. The temperature in this region averages about 85° all year long. Rainfall ranges from 50-120 inches per year.

The Amazon River contains many varieties of fish, including the flesh-eating piranha and the pirarucu, one of the largest fish found in South America. The basin region of the Amazon contains creatures such as alligators, anacondas, parrots and thousands of unusual insects.

The first complete descent of the Amazon was made by an expedition led by Gonzalo Pizarro, in 1541.

Pizarro, a Spaniard, had sailed with Christopher Columbus on his discovery voyage to America. His expedition set out from the Andes with over 4,000 Indian slaves to search for the fabled city of El Dorado. One of the members of the expedition, Francisco de Orellana, left the group in the tropical rain forest as he went ahead looking for food and supplies. Orellana never went back, and eight months later he came to the mouth of the Amazon River.

In 1637, an expedition from Portugal explored the Amazon by traveling up the river to its source.

Almost three centuries later, the first scientific exploration of the Amazon was made by the Victorian naturalists, Alfred Wallace and Henry Bates.

Even though there is not a single bridge that crosses the Amazon River for its entire course, the Amazon basin has been opened to outsiders by other modern developments. The most important development is a series of landing strips cut into the thick jungles that link the isolated people to larger communities and cities through air transportation.

• Write how the planes have changed life for people living along the Amazon.

Page 99

Write, check. Name_____

The Amazon River

...is the greatest **river system** in the world.

...is ☑ 4,000 ☐ 40,000 miles long.

...contains more water than the **Nile** , the **Yangtze** , and the **Mississippi** Rivers together.

...is only surpassed in length by the **Nile** River.

...drains over **2,500,000** square miles of land.

...empties into the **Atlantic** Ocean at a rate of ☐ one ☑ three billion gallons of water a minute.

...is over **200** miles wide at its mouth.

The Amazon River begins as the **Apurimac** River, high in the **Andes** Mountains of ☑ Peru ☐ Colombia in South America.

The river flows ☐ westward ☑ eastward through Brazil.

Much of the Amazon River...
☑ covers an area that makes up the world's largest tropical rainforest.
☐ covers an area of dry, barren desert.

The tropical rainforest averages **85°** degrees, with **50** to **120** inches of rainfall per year.

Name 2 kinds of fish found in the Amazon River.
flesh-eating piranha **pirarucu**

Name 4 kinds of animals found in the basin region of the Amazon.
alligators **anacondas** **parrots** **insects**

The word expedition means:
☐ a scientific laboratory.
☑ a journey for exploration.

The first complete descent of the Amazon River was made by an expedition led by **Gonzalo Pizarro** in 1541.

Pizarro had sailed with **Columbus** on his discovery voyage to America.

One of the members of the expedition, **Francisco de Orellana** left the group to look for ☑ food ☐ gold ☑ supplies

Orellana reached the mouth of the Amazon River **eight** months later.

Underline the sentence that tells which expedition explored the Amazon by traveling up the river.

Answer Key

Page 92

Wonder About:

Antarctica

Name_____

One of the most incredible natural wonders in the world is Antarctica, the continent surrounding the South Pole. It contains 90 percent of the world's ice. Antarctica, the coldest and most desolate region on Earth, covers 5,400,000 square miles. Much of the land is buried under snow and ice one mile thick. Mountains of ice, called glaciers, move slowly across the land to the sea. The winter temperatures reach −100°F in the interior of the continent. On the coast, the temperatures fall below −40°F. This frozen land lies over 600 miles from the tip of South America, the nearest land. New Zealand is 2,100 miles away and South Africa, 2,500 miles.

The interior of Antarctica is a frozen, lifeless region. The only animal life in Antarctica is found on the coastline or in the sea. Penguins, seals, whales and other fish and birds live in or close to the coastal waters. These animals all live on food from the sea.

The ancient Greeks called the North Pole, the Arctic. They believed that land at the South Pole must also exist. They called this supposed land, Antarctica, meaning the opposite of Arctic.

Through the centuries, hunters and whalers may have discovered this land. But in 1838, Lieutenant Charles Wilkes of the United States Navy, was sent to investigate this southern land. He reported back that the land was indeed large enough to be a continent. This opened up the way for explorers to study the region. But after several years, interest in Antarctica began to fade.

In 1928, Commander Richard E. Byrd of the U.S. Navy led a famous expedition to the South Pole. He and his men set up a base called Little America. On November 28, 1929, Byrd and his companions became the first men to fly over the South Pole. Until his death in 1957, Byrd took five expeditions to Antarctica. He helped establish scientific research bases and led the largest Antarctic expedition in history with over 4,000 men and 13 ships. The expedition was called Operation Highjump.

From July 1, 1957, to December 31, 1958, twelve nations joined together to explore and conduct research in Antarctica. The effort occurred during the International Geophysical Year (IGY). This effort involved over 10,000 men operating from over 40 research stations.

During IGY, the United States operated seven stations. Four of the stations have become permanent bases on Antarctica.

• Find three discoveries which were made in the Antarctica during the IGY.

Page 93

Write, check.

Name_____

Antarctica

...is the continent which surrounds the **South** Pole.

...contains ☐ 50 ☑ 90 percent of the world's ice.

...is the ☑ coldest ☐ largest and most desolate region on Earth.

...covers **5,400,000** square miles.

...has a **1** -mile thick covering of snow and ice over much of its land.

...has a winter temperature of **−100°** F in the interior of the land.

...has a coastal temperature which falls below **−40°** F.

...lies over ☐ 6000 ☑ 600 miles from the tip of **South** America, the nearest land.

Write, check.

The ancient Greeks called the North Pole, the **Arctic** .

They believed that ☑ there must be land at the South Pole, too. ☐ there must be a West Pole.

The Greeks called this supposed land **Antarctica** .

In 1838, Lieutenant **Charles Wilkes** of the United States Navy was sent ☐ to Greece. ☑ to investigate Antarctica.

Write, check.

In 1928, Commander **Richard E. Byrd** of the United States Navy led an expedition to the South Pole.

Byrd and his crew . . .

...set up a base called **Little America** .

...became the first men to fly over the **South Pole** , on November **28** , 19 **29** .

...made ☐ two ☑ five expeditions to Antarctica.

...led the largest expedition in history, called Operation **Highjump** with over **4000** men and **13** ships.

IGY stands for

International G eophysical Y ear .

Page 94

Wonder About:

Mount Everest

Name_____

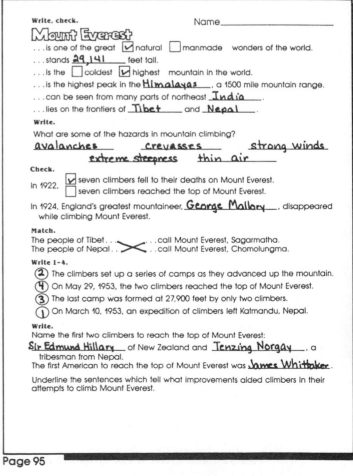

Indian Ocean

Mount Everest is one of the great natural wonders of the world. At 29,141 feet, it stands as the highest mountain in the world. Mount Everest is the highest peak in the Himalayas, a 1500 mile mountain range. Mount Everest can be seen from many parts of northeast India. It lies on the frontiers of Tibet and Nepal, north of India.

Mount Everest was named for Sir George Everest, a British surveyor-general of India. The people of Tibet call Mount Everest, Chomolungma. The people of Nepal call it Sagarmatha.

Through the years, many people tried to climb Mount Everest. The attempts were made hazardous by avalanches, crevasses, strong winds, extreme steepness and thin air. In 1922, seven climbers fell to their deaths on the slopes of the northeast ridge of Mount Everest, called the North Col. In 1924, George Mallory, England's greatest mountaineer, disappeared while trying to climb Mount Everest.

On March 10, 1953, an expedition of climbers left Katmandu, Nepal. They climbed the south side of the mountain, which had previously been called unclimbable. The climbers set up a series of camps as they advanced up the mountain. Few people were able to go to each new camp as they continued to climb. The last camp was formed at 27,900 feet by only two climbers. On May 29, 1953, the two climbers reached the top of Mount Everest. They were Sir Edmund Hillary of New Zealand, and Tenzing Norgay, a tribesman from Nepal.

In 1956, an expedition of climbers from Switzerland reached the summit of Mount Everest. They also were the first climbers to reach the top of Lhotse, the fourth highest peak in the world.

On May 1, 1963, James Whittaker became the first American to reach the top of Mount Everest. Other members of this expedition reached the top on May 22nd.

The ascent of Mount Everest became obtainable by the use of specialized clothing and gear designed to endure the extreme weather conditions. Also, oxygen equipment developed during World War II, provided a defense against the thin air at high altitudes.

Mount Everest has been climbed by expeditions from England, Switzerland, America, Italy, China, Poland, India and Japan, among others.

• Find the name of the second highest mountain in the world.

Page 95

Write, check.

Name_____

Mount Everest

...is one of the great ☑ natural ☐ manmade wonders of the world.

...stands **29,141** feet tall.

...is the ☐ coldest ☑ highest mountain in the world.

...is the highest peak in the **Himalayas** , a 1500 mile mountain range.

...can be seen from many parts of northeast **India** .

...lies on the frontiers of **Tibet** and **Nepal** .

Write.

What are some of the hazards in mountain climbing?

avalanches **crevasses** **strong winds** **extreme steepness** **thin air**

Check.

In 1922, ☑ seven climbers fell to their deaths on Mount Everest. ☐ seven climbers reached the top of Mount Everest.

In 1924, England's greatest mountaineer, **George Mallory** , disappeared while climbing Mount Everest.

Match.

The people of Tibet . . . . . .call Mount Everest, Sagarmatha.
The people of Nepal . . . . . .call Mount Everest, Chomolungma.

Write 1-4.

② The climbers set up a series of camps as they advanced up the mountain.

④ On May 29, 1953, the two climbers reached the top of Mount Everest.

③ The last camp was formed at 27,900 feet by only two climbers.

① On March 10, 1953, an expedition of climbers left Katmandu, Nepal.

Write.

Name the first two climbers to reach the top of Mount Everest:

Sir Edmund Hillary of New Zealand and **Tenzing Norgay** , a tribesman from Nepal.

The first American to reach the top of Mount Everest was **James Whittaker** .

Underline the sentences which tell what improvements aided climbers in their attempts to climb Mount Everest.
